POLITICAL PARTIES, INTEREST GROUPS
AND ELECTIONS

POLITICAL PARTIES, INTEREST GROUPS AND ELECTIONS

EDITED BY BRIAN DUIGNAN, SENIOR EDITOR, RELIGION AND PHILOSOPHY

Britannica
Educational Publishing

IN ASSOCIATION WITH

ROSEN
EDUCATIONAL SERVICES

Published in 2013 by Britannica Educational Publishing
(a trademark of Encyclopædia Britannica, Inc.)
in association with Rosen Educational Services, LLC
29 East 21st Street, New York, NY 10010

First Edition

Britannica Educational Publishing
J.E. Luebering: Senior Manager
Adam Augustyn: Assistant Manager
Marilyn L. Barton: Senior Coordinator, Production Control
Steven Bosco: Director, Editorial Technologies
Lisa S. Braucher: Senior Producer and Data Editor
Yvette Charboneau: Senior Copy Editor
Kathy Nakamura: Manager, Media Acquisition
Brian Duignan: Senior Editor, Religion and Philosophy

Rosen Educational Services
Jeanne Nagle: Senior Editor
Nelson Sá: Art Director
Cindy Reiman: Photography Manager
Brian Garvey: Designer, Cover Design
Introduction by Michael Levy

Library of Congress Cataloging-in-Publication Data

Political parties, interest groups, and elections/Edited by Brian Duignan.—First edition.
    pages cm.—(Governance: power, politics, and participation)
Includes bibliographical references and index.
ISBN 978-1-61530-703-6 (library binding)
1. Political parties. 2. Pressure groups. 3. Elections. I. Duignan, Brian.
JF2051.P577 2012
324—dc23

2011053231

Manufactured in the United States of America

On the cover, pp. i, iii (top): State delegates on the floor of the 1996 Democratic National
Convention hall in Chicago. *Paula Bronstein/Stone/Getty Images*

On the cover (center), pp. i (center), iii (center), 1, 41, 72, 93, 137, 140, 142, 145: Columns
that make up the portico of the United States Supreme Court. © *www.istockphoto.com/Jeremy
Edwards*

On the cover, pp. i, iii (bottom): A crowd celebrating an apparent victory. © *www.istock-
photo.com/Moodboard Images*

CONTENTS

8

42

55

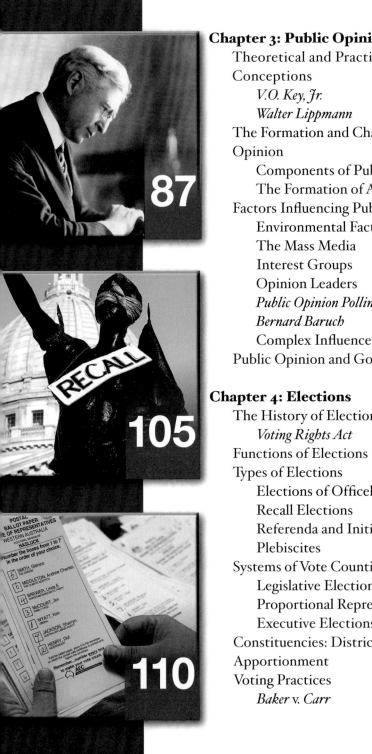

124

130

INTRODUCTION

What defines a democratic country is that citizens are free to form associations to lobby government on behalf of their interests and form political parties that seek to control government through free and fair elections. Elections themselves can be found in almost every country around the world. But does that mean that all countries that hold elections are democracies? Simply put, no.

In some countries, elections are mere window dressing, the outcome a foregone conclusion, with those

holding power placing restrictions on parties and people that can run—and sometimes stuffing the ballot box for good measure. In Myanmar, for example, the military government held a free election in 1990, but when the opposition won an overwhelming victory, the authorities simply ignored the results. Likewise, in Egypt and Tunisia, before the events of the Arab Spring of 2011, longstanding governments consistently won elections, sometimes with upwards of 90 percent of the vote or more. In these contests, however, the right of opposition groups to participate and campaign was severely curtailed, and the fragility of the regimes was obvious when their governments were swept from power quickly by popular mass demonstrations.

In some democratic countries, elections may be free and fair but not very competitive, at least for long periods. In post–World War II Japan, for example, opposition groups could participate unfettered, but one party, the Liberal-Democratic Party, maintained power for almost all of the period from 1955 until it was ousted by the opposition Democratic Party of Japan in 2009. Even in the United States, Republicans held an almost iron grip on the White House from 1861 to 1933, holding the presidency for 56 of the 72 years until the Great Depression ushered in an era of Democratic ascendency that would last for more than three decades.

Voting is the most basic right of citizens in democratic countries, but there is wide variation in how many people actually turn out to the polls. In some countries, such as Australia, Austria, Belgium, Chile, Indonesia, Italy, and Portugal, voter turnout often exceeds 85 percent of the voting age population for national elections, while in others, such as Brazil, Mexico, Poland, Switzerland, and the United States, turnout rates are about 50 percent. There are various reasons that explain why countries have higher or lower voter turnout. In those countries with high voter turnout rates, voting is sometimes compulsory, registration is the responsibility of the government (rather than individuals, as in the United States), and voting may take place on the weekends (when fewer people work). Paradoxically, helping to reduce voter turnout rates in the United States and Switzerland is that in both countries voters vote on a great many issues in frequent elections. There are some estimates that there are more than 500,000 elected state and local officials in the United

States. In addition, Americans vote on all manner of referenda and initiatives. Likewise, in Switzerland, there is a tradition of direct democracy, with voters casting binding decisions on issues from the local to the federal constitutional levels. It is thought that the overwhelming number of elections increases the information costs to voters, influencing some to abstain from voting.

When it comes to voting in the United States, the refrain is often "I don't vote for the party, I vote for the person." True enough, voters in the United States do not specifically choose among competing parties—in many other countries, voters do cast ballots for political parties rather than candidates—but that hardly means that political parties are unimportant to the outcome of elections. Political parties aggregate the interests of some groups of people in society. In countries with a two-party system, such as the United States, political parties generally espouse a wide array of positions that seek to appeal to diverse segments of society. In countries with multiparty systems, a political party might appeal to a very narrow segment of the population—such as the Pirate Party, which seeks reform of patent and copyright law and which won nearly 9 percent of the vote in state elections in Berlin, Germany, in September 2011.

Because there are limited choices for voters in a two-party system, individuals sometimes feel frustrated because they support and oppose some aspects of each party's and each candidate's policies. Once you go beyond the marquee electoral contests, such as president of the United States or governor of a state, the information that voters have about individual candidates diminishes, increasing the importance of general political party affiliation. As citizens cast their votes for "down ballot" races, such as for judges or aldermen, political party serves as a device for individuals who often cast their choice based not on full information about the various candidates, but with a general understanding that the candidates of each party are likely to support a particular general set of principles.

But why does America have a two-party system? Since the 1850s, America's two-party system has consisted of the Democratic and Republican parties. Third parties have sometimes risen to prominence, such as in the 1912 presidential election, when Bull Moose candidate Theodore Roosevelt won second place, or in 1992, when Ross Perot amassed nearly one in five votes competing against Republican George H. W. Bush and Democrat Bill Clinton. Still, these cases have been rare and their "success" limited to presidential politics. While Roosevelt and Perot were running for the presidency, they did not form cohesive political organizations behind them that contested seats in the House of Representatives and Senate.

There are several reasons why the Democratic and Republican parties have been able to maintain their dominance over the political system. First is ballot access. The Democrats and Republicans generally have automatic access to the ballot, whereas third-party candidates generally have to gather a large number of signatures to qualify for a place on the general election ballot. Collecting these signatures does not just take time; it takes money and organization, things that incipient third parties generally do not have. Even if third parties qualify for a spot on the ballot, they often find themselves locked out of political debates, thus debilitating their candidates from gaining name recognition and having their ideas heard.

As mentioned, money also is a major obstacle for third parties. The Democratic and Republican parties, by virtue of their control over the levers of power, are able to raise vast amounts of money, while individuals who might be sympathetic to a third-party candidate, particularly wealthier donors who want to have an influence over legislation, may not want to "waste" their hard-earned money on a candidate with very little chance of winning.

Perhaps most important, the American electoral system generally favors the formation of two large parties. Members of Congress are elected to their seats in what are called single-member districts. In the House of Representatives, for example, there are 435 members of Congress, with seats broken into 435 separate districts. In each of those districts, the person with the most votes wins. While that might seem obvious, it is but one method of election, and one that generally helps larger political parties.

Let's say, for example, that a third party gains access to the ballot, can participate in debates, and even is able to raise enough money to wage a credible political campaign. To win election, that candidate is now going to need to gain more votes than either the Democrat or Republican candidate. Easy, right? Not very. The two major parties start with a partisan advantage; polls generally show that a majority of Americans consider themselves either Democrats or Republicans. The remainder of voters consider themselves independent (or do not generally vote), but even among independents, many actually vote consistently as either Democrats or Republicans. A third-party candidate thus must win almost all the people who consider themselves neither Democrats nor Republicans—a fairly tall order.

Even if a third party did do relatively well in capturing votes, the fact that there are 435 separate Congressional districts makes it unlikely that it will gain many seats. For example, if a third party received 10 percent of the vote in every district in Congress, that party would likely win zero seats. The same is true in presidential elections. For the electoral college, most states operate on a winner-take-all system, whereby the winner of that state's popular votes wins all of that state's electoral votes. In 1992 Ross Perot garnered 19 percent of the popular vote, but in no state did he win the most votes, so he won zero electoral votes. Contrast that result to Strom Thurmond, a Dixiecrat candidate for president in 1948. Appealing largely to Democrats in the South who had been alienated by the national Democratic Party, Thurmond won 2.4 percent of the national vote, but he won 39 electoral votes, winning the most votes in four states. This suggests that while third parties generally do not perform well in two-party systems with single-member district elections, third parties with geographically concentrated support can actually do well.

Not all countries with a single-member district electoral system have only two parties. Canada and the United Kingdom, which have electoral systems similar to those in the United States, generally have had two large parties and several minor ones. Some of those minor parties may be national in scope, such as the Liberal Democrats in the United Kingdom, but others are typically regionally concentrated, such as the Scottish National Party in the United Kingdom and the Bloc Québécois in Canada.

In some countries, multiple parties are encouraged by the electoral system. For example, the Netherlands and Israel have proportional representation electoral systems, in which voters choose parties rather than individual candidates. In recent elections in both countries, 10 or more parties have won seats in the fairly small legislatures (120 seats in Israel and 150 in the Netherlands). Because of the large number of parties in these systems, it is unlikely that any single party will gain a majority to form a government, meaning that parties with even a small number of seats can influence policy and enter government.

If political parties and elections are the vehicles through which citizens in democracies can directly assert control over government at regular intervals, it is through interest groups that citizens can influence the legislative process once governments are formed. We often hear the phrase *special interests* to describe the role that interest groups (sometimes called pressure groups) play in the political process—and the term *special* is usually used to convey something negative or even sinister. But, what is a special interest to one person may be simply a like-minded group to another, and what defines special in one sense is an interest with which one disagrees. Interest groups are vital to democracies because they aggregate the diverse views that exist in the broader public, and on behalf of that interest lobby government officials to pass legislation to benefit themselves or their causes.

There are an almost infinite number of interests that might organize themselves. Some represent economic interests (e.g., business, labour, and professional organizations), others promote particular general values, and still others may represent the public interest at large. They may organize broadly—for example, the People for the American Way represents liberal interests while the American Conservative Union promotes conservative causes. Conversely, they may promote single causes—for example, the National Abortion Rights Action League and the National Right to Life Committee, which supports and opposes abortion rights, respectively

Interest groups engage in what is called lobbying, which entails trying to influence the votes of legislators. Groups with extensive resources are likely to be able to pursue so-called "inside lobbying" strategies, directly lobbying legislators and providing them with information and expertise to influence their positions. When individual members of Congress retire or lose office, they may be hired as lobbyists so that they can take advantage of their close contacts with their former colleagues. Groups that may not have such close contacts or money may use "outside lobbying" strategies to influence legislators; for example, they may engage in grassroots activities such as letter writing and e-mail or Internet campaigns, or hold public demonstrations to gain favourable media coverage in an attempt to sway public opinion in their favor.

Political parties, interest groups, and elections each are necessary for democracy to thrive. But simply because a country holds elections and has political parties and groups that may resemble interest groups does not mean that it is a democracy. Keep in mind that what defines a democracy is that citizens are able to form political parties and interest groups, even when they vehemently oppose the government, and that elections are free and fair.

CHAPTER 1

Political Parties

A political party is a group of people organized to acquire and exercise political power. Political parties originated in their modern form in Europe and the United States in the 19th century, along with the electoral and parliamentary systems, whose development reflects the evolution of parties. The term *party* has since come to be applied to all organized groups seeking political power, whether by democratic elections or by revolution.

In earlier, prerevolutionary, aristocratic and monarchical regimes, the political process unfolded within restricted circles in which cliques and factions, grouped around particular noblemen or influential personalities, were opposed to one another. The establishment of parliamentary regimes and the appearance of parties at first scarcely changed this situation. To cliques formed around princes, dukes, counts, or marquesses there were added cliques formed around bankers, merchants, industrialists, and businessmen. Regimes supported by nobles were succeeded by regimes supported by other elites. These narrowly based parties were later transformed to a greater or lesser extent, for in the 19th century in Europe and America there emerged parties depending on mass support.

The 20th century saw the spread of political parties throughout the entire world. In Africa large parties were sometimes formed in which a modern organization had a more traditional ethnic or tribal basis. In such cases the

Writer Mary Wortley (second from right) *was but a young girl when she was inducted into the Kit-Cat Club, an elite clique of Whig leaders formed in early 18th-century England.* Hulton Archive/ Getty Images

party leadership was frequently made up of tribal chiefs. In certain areas of Asia, membership in modern political parties was often determined largely by religious factors or by affiliation with ritual brotherhoods. Many political parties in developing countries were partly political and partly military. Certain socialist and communist parties in Europe experienced the same tendencies.

These last-mentioned European parties demonstrated an equal aptitude for functioning within multiparty democracies and as the sole political party in a dictatorship. Developing originally within the framework of liberal democracy in the 19th century, political parties have been used in the 20th and 21st centuries by dictatorships for entirely undemocratic purposes.

TYPES OF POLITICAL PARTIES

A fundamental distinction can be made between cadre parties and mass-based parties. The two forms coexist in many countries, particularly in western Europe, where communist and socialist parties emerged alongside the older conservative and liberal parties. Many parties do not fall exactly into either category but combine some characteristics of both.

CADRE PARTIES

Cadre parties—i.e., parties dominated by politically elite groups of activists—developed in Europe and America during the 19th century. Except in some of the states of the United States, France from 1848, and the German Empire from 1871, the suffrage was largely restricted to taxpayers and property owners, and, even when the right to vote was given to larger numbers of people, political influence was essentially limited to a very small segment of the population. The mass of people were limited to the role of spectators rather than that of active participants.

The cadre parties of the 19th century reflected a fundamental conflict between two classes: the aristocracy on the one hand and the bourgeoisie on the other. The former, composed of landowners, depended upon rural estates on which a generally unlettered peasantry was held back by a traditionalist clergy. The bourgeoisie, made up of industrialists, merchants, tradesmen, bankers, financiers, and professional people, depended upon the lower classes of clerks and industrial workers in the cities.

Both aristocracy and bourgeoisie evolved its own ideology. Bourgeois liberal ideology developed first, originating at the time of the English revolution of the 17th century in the writings of John Locke, an English philosopher. It was then developed by French philosophers of the 18th century. In its clamouring for formal legal equality and acceptance of the inequities of circumstance, liberal ideology reflected the interests of the bourgeoisie, who wished to destroy the privileges of the aristocracy and eliminate the lingering economic restraints of feudalism and mercantilism. But, insofar as it set forth an egalitarian ideal and a demand for liberty, bourgeois classical liberalism expressed aspirations common to all citizens.

Conservative ideology, on the other hand, never succeeded in defining themes that would prove as attractive, for it appeared to be more closely allied to the interests of the aristocracy. For a considerable period, however, conservative sentiment did maintain a considerable impact among the people, since it was presented as the expression of the will of God. In Roman Catholic countries, in which religion was based upon a hierarchically structured and authoritarian clergy, the conservative parties were often the clerical parties, as in France, Italy, and Belgium.

Conservative and liberal cadre parties dominated European politics in the 19th century. Developing during a period of great social and economic upheaval, they exercised power largely through electoral and parliamentary activity. Once in power, their leaders used the power of the army or of the police; the party itself was not generally organized for violent activity. Its local units were charged with assuring moral and financial backing to candidates at election time, as well as with maintaining continual contact between elected officials and the electorate. The national organization endeavoured to unify the party members who had been elected to the assemblies. In general, the local committees maintained a basic autonomy and each legislator a large measure of independence. The party discipline in voting established by the British parties—which were older because of the fact that the British

Pope Pius IX, head of the Roman Catholic Church, 1846–78. Originally a moderate liberal, Pius adopted a more conservative approach to his papal rule following the Revolutions of 1848. Hulton Archive/Getty Images

Parliament was long established—was imitated on the Continent hardly at all.

The first United States political parties of the 19th century were not particularly different from European cadre parties, except that their confrontations were less violent and based less on ideology. The first American form of the struggle between the aristocracy and the bourgeoisie, between conservative and liberal, was carried out in the form of the Revolutionary War, in which Great Britain embodied the power of the king and the nobility, and the insurgents that of bourgeoisie and liberalism. Such an interpretation is, of course, simplified. There were some aristocrats in the South and, in particular, an aristocratic spirit based on the institutions of slaveholding and paternalistic ownership of land. In this sense, the Civil War could be considered as a second phase of violent conflict between the conservatives and the liberals. Nevertheless, the United States was from the beginning an essentially bourgeois civilization, based on a deep sense of equality and of individual freedom. Federalists and Anti-Federalists, Republicans and Democrats—all belonged to the liberal family since all shared the same basic ideology and the same system of fundamental values and differed only in the means by which they would realize their beliefs.

In terms of party structure, United States parties in the beginning differed little from their European counterparts. Like them, the United States parties were composed of local notables. The ties of a local committee to a national organization were even weaker than in Europe. At the state level there was some effective coordination of local party organizations, but at the national level such coordination did not exist. A more original structure was developed after the Civil War—in the South to exploit the vote of African Americans and along the East Coast to control the votes of immigrants.

The extreme decentralization in the United States enabled a party to establish a local quasi-dictatorship in a city or county by capturing all of the key posts in an election. Not only the position of mayor but also the police, finances, and the courts came under the control of the party machine, and the machine was thus a development of the original cadre parties. The local party committee came typically to be composed of adventurers or gangsters who wanted to control the distribution of wealth and to ensure the continuation of their control. These people were themselves controlled by the power of the boss, the political leader who controlled the machine at the city, county, or state levels. At the direction of the committee, each constituency was carefully divided, and every precinct was watched closely by an agent of the party, the captain, who was responsible for securing votes for the party. Various rewards were offered to voters in return for the promise of their votes. The machine could offer such inducements as union jobs, trader's licences, immunity from the police, and the like. Operating in this manner, a party could frequently guarantee a majority in an election to the candidates of its choosing, and, once it was in control of local government—including the police, the courts, and public finances—the machine and its clients were assured of impunity in illicit activities such as prostitution and gambling rings and the granting of public contracts to favoured businessmen.

The degeneration of the party mechanism was not without benefits. The European immigrant who arrived in the United States lost and isolated in a huge and different world might find work and lodging in return for his commitment to the party. In a system of almost pure capitalism and at a time when social services were practically nonexistent, machines and bosses took upon themselves responsibilities that were indispensable to community

Cartoon of William Magear Tweed, with a money bag for a head. "Boss" Tweed ran the corrupt political machine that gained millions of dollars illegally from New York City in the 1860s. Kean Collection/Archive Photos/Getty Images

life. But the moral and material cost of such a system was very high, and the machine was often purely exploitative, performing no services to the community.

By the end of the 19th century the excesses of the machines and the bosses and the closed character of the parties led to the development of primary elections, in which party nominees for office were selected. The primary movement deprived party leaders of the right to dictate candidates for election. A majority of the states adopted the primary system in one form or another between 1900 and 1920. The aim of the system was to make the parties more democratic by opening them up to the general public in the hope of counterbalancing the influence of the party committees. In practice, the aim was not realized, for the committees retained the upper hand in the selection of candidates for the primaries.

In its original form, the British Labour Party constituted a new type of cadre party, forming an intermediate link with the mass-based parties. It was formed with the support of trade unions and left-wing intellectuals. At the base, each local organization sent representatives to a district labour committee, which was in turn represented at the national congress.

The early (pre-1918) Labour Party was thus structured of many local and regional organizations. It was not possible to join the party directly; membership came only through an affiliated body, such as a trade union. It thus represented a new type of party, depending not upon highly political individuals brought together as a result of their desire to acquire and wield power but upon the organized representatives of a broader interest—the working class. Certain Christian Democratic parties—the Belgian Social Christian Party between the two world wars and the Austrian Popular Party, for example—had an analogous structure, with a federation of unions, agricultural organizations, middle class movements, employers' associations, and so on. After 1918, the Labour Party developed a policy of direct membership on the model of the continental socialist parties, individual members being permitted to join local-constituency branches. The majority of its membership, however, continued to be affiliated rather than direct.

MASS-BASED PARTIES

Cadre parties normally organize a relatively small number of party adherents. Mass-based parties, on the other hand, unite hundreds of thousands of followers, sometimes millions. But the number of members is not the only criterion of a mass-based party. The essential factor is that such a party attempts to base itself on an appeal to the masses. It attempts to organize not only those who are influential or well known or those who represent special interest groups but rather any citizen who is willing to join the party. If such a party succeeds in gathering only a few adherents, then it is mass based only in potential. It remains, nevertheless, different from the cadre-type parties.

At the end of the 19th century the socialist parties of continental Europe organized themselves on a mass basis in order to educate and organize the growing population of labourers and wage earners—which industrialization was making increasingly large and which was becoming more important politically because of extensions of the suffrage—and to gather the money necessary for propaganda by mobilizing in a regular fashion the resources of those who, although poor, were numerous. Membership campaigns were conducted, and each member paid party dues. If its members became sufficiently numerous, the party emerged as a powerful organization, managing large funds and diffusing its ideas among an important segment of the population. Such was the case with the German Social Democratic Party, which by 1913 had more than one million members.

Such organizations were necessarily rigidly structured. The party required an exact registration of membership, treasurers to collect dues, secretaries to call and lead local meetings, and a hierarchical framework for the coordination of the thousands of local sections. A tradition of collective action and group discipline, more developed among workers as a result of their participation in strikes and other union activity, favoured the development and centralization of party organization.

A complex party organization tends to give a great deal of influence to those who have responsibility at various levels in the hierarchy, resulting in certain oligarchical tendencies. The socialist parties made an effort to control this tendency by developing democratic procedures in the choice of leaders. At every level, those in responsible positions were elected by members of the party. Every local party group would elect delegates to regional and national congresses, at which party candidates and party leaders would be chosen and party policy decided.

The type of mass-based party described above was imitated by many nonsocialist parties. Some cadre-type parties in Europe, both conservative and liberal, attempted to transform themselves along similar lines. The Christian Democratic parties often developed organizations copied even more directly from the mass-based model. But nonsocialist parties were generally less successful in establishing rigid and disciplined organizations.

The first communist parties were splinter groups of existing socialist parties and at first adopted the organization of these parties. After 1924, as a result of a decision of the Comintern (the Third International, or federation of working class parties), all communist parties were

COMMUNIST PARTY

A communist party is a political party organized to facilitate the transition of society from capitalism through socialism to communism. Russia was the first country in which communists came to power (1917). In 1918 the Bolshevik party was renamed the All-Russian Communist Party. The name was taken to distinguish its members from the socialists of the Second International, who had supported capitalist governments during World War I. Its basic unit was the workers' council (soviet), above which were district, city, regional, and republic committees. At the top was the party congress, which met only every few years. The delegates of the congress elected the members of the Central Committee, who in turn elected the members of the Politburo and the Secretariat, though those organizations were actually largely self-perpetuating.

The Soviet Union dominated communist parties worldwide through World War II. Yugoslavia challenged that hegemony in 1948, and China went its own way starting in the 1950s. Communist parties have survived the demise of the Soviet Union (1991) but with much-reduced political influence. Cuba's party remains in control, as does a hereditary communist party in North Korea.

transformed along the lines of the Soviet model, becoming mass parties based on the membership of the largest possible number of citizens, although membership was limited to those who embraced and espoused the ideology of Marxism-Leninism.

The communist parties developed a new structural organization: whereas the local committees of cadre and socialist parties focused their organizing efforts and drew their support from a particular geographical area, communist groups formed their cells in the place of work. The

Russian farmers attending a collective farm meeting in 1941. The communist party drew strength in the early 20th century by organizing political cells within existing workplace or social groups.
Margaret Bourke-White/Time & Life Pictures/Getty Images

workplace cell was the first original element in communist party organization. It grouped together all party members who depended upon the same firm, workshop, or store or the same professional institution (school or university, for example). Party members thus tended to be tightly organized, their solidarity, resulting from a common occupation, being stronger than that based upon residence.

The workplace-cell system proved to be effective, and other parties tried to imitate it, generally without success. Such an organization led each cell to concern itself with problems of a corporate and professional nature rather than with those of a more political nature. However, these basic groups, which were smaller and therefore more numerous than the socialist sections, tended to go their separate ways. It was necessary to have a very strong party structure and for party leaders to have extensive authority if the groups were to resist such centrifugal pressure.

This resulted in a second distinctive characteristic of the communist parties, which was a high degree of centralization. Although all mass-based parties tended to be centralized, communist parties were more so than others. There was, in principle, free discussion, which was supposedly developed at every level before a decision was made, but afterward all were required to adhere to the decision that had been made by the central body. The splintering that had from time to time divided or paralyzed the socialist parties was forbidden in communist parties, which generally succeeded in maintaining their unity.

A further distinctive characteristic of communist parties was the importance given to ideology. All parties had a doctrine, or at least a platform. The European socialist parties, which were doctrinaire before 1914 and between the two world wars, later became more pragmatic. But, in communist parties, ideology occupied a much more fundamental place, a primary concern of the party being to indoctrinate its members in Marxism.

The 1920s and '30s saw the emergence of fascist parties that attempted, as did the communist and socialist parties, to organize the maximum number of members but that did not claim to represent the great masses of people. Their teaching was authoritarian and elitist. They thought that societies should be directed by the most talented and capable people—by an elite. The party leadership, grouped under the absolute authority of a supreme head, constituted such an elite. Party structure had as its goal the assurance of the obedience of the elite.

This structure resembled that of armies, which are also organized in such a way as to ensure, by means of rigorous discipline, the obedience of a large number of soldiers to an elite leadership. The party structure, therefore, made use of a military-type organization, consisting of a pyramid made up of units that at the base were very tiny but that, when joined with other units, formed groups that got larger and larger. Uniforms, ranks, orders, salutes, marches, and unquestioning obedience were all aspects of fascist parties. This similarity rests upon another factor: namely, that fascist doctrine taught that power must be seized by organized minorities making use of force. The party thus made use of a militia intended to assure victory in the struggle for control over the unorganized masses.

Large parties built upon the fascist model developed between the two world wars in Italy and Germany, where they actually came to power. Fascist parties appeared also in most other countries of western Europe during this period but were unable to achieve power. The less-developed nations of eastern Europe and Latin America were equally infected by the movement. The victory of the Allies in World War II, as well as the revelation of the horrors of Nazism, temporarily stopped the growth of the fascists and provoked their decline. In the decades after the war, however, neofascist political parties and movements, which had much in common with their fascist forebears, arose in several European countries, though by the early 21st century none had come to power.

PARTIES AND POLITICAL POWER

Whether they are conservative or revolutionary, whether they are a union of notables or an organization of the masses, whether they function in a pluralistic democracy or in a monolithic dictatorship, parties have one function in common. They all participate to some extent in the exercise of political power, whether by forming a government or by exercising the function of opposition, a function that is often of crucial importance in the determination of national policy.

THE STRUGGLE FOR POWER

It is possible in theory to distinguish revolutionary parties, which attempt to gain power by violence (conspiracies, guerrilla warfare, and so on), from those parties working within the legal framework of elections. But the distinction is not always easy to make, because the same parties may sometimes make use of both procedures, either simultaneously or successively, depending upon the circumstances. In the 1920s, for example, communist parties sought power through elections at the same time that they were developing an underground activity of a revolutionary nature. In the 19th century, liberal parties were in the same situation, sometimes employing the techniques of conspiracy, as in Italy, Austria, Germany, Poland, and Russia, and sometimes confining their struggles to the ballot box, as in Great Britain and France.

Revolutionary methods vary greatly. Clandestine plots by which minority groups seize the centres of power presuppose monarchies or dictatorships in which the masses of people have little say in government. But terrorist and disruptive activity can serve to mobilize citizens and to demonstrate the powerlessness of any government. At the beginning of the 20th century leftist trade unionists extolled the revolutionary general strike, a total stoppage of all economic activity that would paralyze society completely and put the government at the revolutionaries' mercy. Rural guerrilla activity has often been used in countries with a predominantly agrarian society. Urban guerrilla warfare was effective in the European revolutions of the

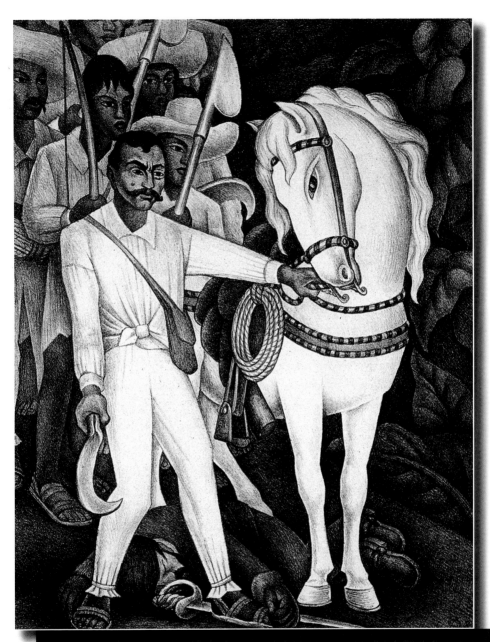

Portrait of Mexican revolutionary Emiliano Zapata (1879–1919), by Diego Rivera. The scythe in his hand represents Zapata's work toward agrarian reform, which he often accomplished using guerrilla tactics. MPI/Archive Photos/Getty Images

19th century, but the development of techniques of police and military control has made such activity more difficult.

Revolutionary parties are less numerous than parties that work within the law: the contest at election time is the means normally used in the struggle for power. Such activity corresponds, moreover, to the original nature of political parties and involves three factors: (1) the organization of propaganda, (2) the selection of candidates, and (3) the financing of campaigns. The first function is the most visible. The party first of all gives the candidate a label that serves to introduce him to the voters and to identify his position. Because of this party label the voters are better able to distinguish the candidates. The promises and declarations of individuals are seldom taken with too much seriousness, and it means more to indicate that one candidate is a communist, another a socialist, a third a fascist, a fourth a liberal, and a fifth a conservative. Finally, the party also furnishes the candidate with workers to raise funds, put up his posters, distribute his literature, organize his meetings, and canvass from door to door.

The function of selecting candidates is exercised in three ways. In cadre parties, candidates are selected by committees of the party activists who make up the party—the caucus system, as it is known in the United States. In general, local committees play essential roles in this regard. In some countries, however, the selection is centralized by a national caucus, such as the Conservative Party in Britain and the Rally for the Republic (1976–2002) in France. In mass-based parties, selection is made by members of the regional and national congresses according to apparently democratic procedures. In actual practice, the governing committees play an essential role, the local constituency members generally ratifying their choice. Thirdly, in the United States the mechanism of primary elections has established a system for selecting candidates by means of the votes of all party members or all voters within a particular electoral district.

The various processes of selecting candidates do not, however, differ significantly in their results, for it is almost always the party leaders who play the essential role. This introduces an oligarchical tendency into party politics, a tendency that has not been overcome by the congresses of the mass-based parties or the United States primaries, which provide only a partial limitation on the power of the governing committees.

An important aspect of the struggle for power between political parties is the financing of campaigns. Cadre parties always have in their committees some key figure having connections with the business world who is responsible for collecting gifts from them. In mass-based parties, rather than looking for large sums of money from a few people, leaders gather smaller sums from a large number of people who usually give on a monthly or annual basis. This method has been viewed as one of the distinguishing characteristics of mass-based parties. Sometimes the law intervenes in the financing of elections and of parties. Laws often limit campaign expenses and attempt to restrict the resources of the parties, but they are generally inoperative because it is quite easy to circumvent them. In some countries the state contributes public funds to the parties. At first, such financial participation was limited to expenses for campaigns and was based on the uniform treatment of candidates (as in France), but in Sweden and Finland the state contributes to the general finances of parties.

PARTICIPATION IN POWER

Once a political party has achieved electoral victory, the question arises of how much influence the party is to have on the government. The influence of the party on members in elective office is frequently quite weak. It defines the general lines of their activity, but these lines can be quite hazy, and few decisions are taken in the periodic meetings between officeholders and their party. Each member of the legislature retains personal freedom of action in his participation in debates, in his participation in government, and, especially, in his voting. The party may, of course, attempt to enforce the party line, but parliamentary or congressional members cannot be compelled to vote the way the party wants them to. Such is the situation in the United States, within most of the liberal and conservative European parties, and within cadre parties in general.

The question of how disciplined a party is, of the extent to which it will always present a united front, enables a distinction to be made between what may be termed rigid and flexible parties—that is, between those that attempt always to be united and disciplined, following what is most often an ideologically based party line, and those that, representing a broader range of interests and points of view, form legislatures that are assemblies of individuals rather than of parties.

Whether the parties operating within a particular system will be rigid or flexible depends largely on the constitutional provisions that determine the circumstances in which a government may continue in office. This is clearly illustrated by comparing the situation in the United States with that in Great Britain. In the United States the president and his government continue in office for the constitutionally defined period of four years, regardless of whether or not a majority in the legislature supports him. Since a united party is thus not crucial to the immediate survival of the government, both major parties are able to contain broad coalitions of interests, and votes on issues of major importance frequently split each party. In the

United Kingdom the situation is quite different. There, government can continue in office only so long as it commands a majority in the legislature. A single adverse vote can result in the dissolution of Parliament and a general election. Party discipline and unity are thus of crucial importance, and this fact has far-reaching consequences for the composition, organization, and policies of each party. The consequences of party disunity within such a constitutional framework are well illustrated by the weakness and instability of the governments of the Third (1870–1940) and Fourth (1946–58) French republics.

The distinction between flexible and rigid parties applies equally to parties in power and to those forming the opposition. Votes of censure or of lack of confidence, votes on proposed legislation or on the budget, questions put to ministers or challenges made to them—in short, all the functions of an opposition party—are worked out differently in flexible and rigid party systems.

In flexible party systems the absence of strong discipline is often of great consequence to the opposition party because only rigid parties can constitute an opposition force sufficiently strong to counterbalance the strength of the party in power. At the same time, party discipline permits the opposition to present the public with an alternative to the majority party; the logical consequence of such a situation is Britain's "shadow cabinet," which accustoms the electorate to the idea that a new group is ready to take over the reins of government.

Parties provide, moreover, a channel of communication between opposition legislators and the public. The governing party performs a similar service for the government, although it is less necessary, since the government has at its disposal numerous means of communicating with the public. Opposition parties thus provide a means of expressing negative reaction to decisions of government and proposing alternatives. This role justifies the official recognition given to opposition parties, as is the case in Great Britain and Scandinavia.

POWER AND REPRESENTATION

It is difficult to envisage how representative democracy could function in a large industrialized society without political parties. In order for citizens to be able to make an intelligent choice of representative or president, it is necessary for them to know the real political orientation of each candidate. Party membership provides the clearest indication of this. The programs and promises of each individual candidate are not too significant or informative, because most candidates, in their attempt to gain the most votes, try to avoid difficult subjects. They all tend to speak the same language—that is, to camouflage their real opinions. The fact that one is a socialist, another a conservative, a third a liberal, and a fourth a communist provides a far better clue as to how the candidate will perform when in office. In the legislature the discipline of the party limits the possibility that elected representatives will change their minds and their politics, and thus the party label acts as a sort of guarantee that there will be at least some correspondence between promise and performance. Parties make possible the representation of varying shades of opinion by synthesizing different positions into a stance that each representative adopts to a greater or lesser extent.

But parties, like all organizations, tend to manipulate their members, to bring them under the control of an inner circle of leaders that often perpetuates itself by cooptation. In cadre parties, members are manipulated by powerful committees containing cliques of influential party leaders. In mass-based parties, leaders are chosen by the members, but incumbents are very often re-elected because they control the party apparatus, using it to ensure their continuation in power.

Democratic political systems, while performing the function of representation, thus rest more or less on the competition of rival oligarchies. But these oligarchies consist of political elites that are open to all with political ambition. No modern democracy could function without parties, the oligarchical tendencies of which are best regarded as a necessary evil.

PARTY SYSTEMS

Party systems may be broken down into three broad categories: two-party, multiparty, and single-party. Such a classification is based not merely on the number of parties operating within a particular country but on a variety of distinctive features that the three systems exhibit. Two-party and multiparty systems represent means of organizing political conflict within pluralistic societies and are thus part of the apparatus of democracy. Single parties usually operate in situations in which genuine political conflict is not tolerated. This broad statement is, however, subject to qualification, for although single parties do not usually permit the expression of points of view that are fundamentally opposed to the party line or ideology, there may well be intense conflict within these limits over policy within the party itself. Also, even within a two-party or a multiparty system, debate may become so stymied and a particular coalition of interests so entrenched that the democratic process is seriously compromised.

The distinction between two-party and multiparty systems is not as easily made as it might appear. In any two-party system there are invariably some tiny parties in addition to the two major parties, and there is always the possibility that such small parties might prevent one of the two main parties from gaining a majority of seats in the legislature. This is the case with regard to the Liberal Democrats in Great Britain, for example. Other countries do not fall clearly into either category; thus, Austria and Germany only approximate the two-party system. It is not simply a question of the number of parties that determines the nature of the two-party system; many other elements are of importance, the extent of party discipline in particular.

MULTIPARTY SYSTEMS

In Anglo-Saxon countries there is a tendency to consider the two-party system as normal and the multiparty system as the exceptional case. But, in fact, the two-party system that operates in Great Britain, the United States, and New Zealand is much rarer than the multiparty system, which is found in almost all of Europe.

In Europe, three major categories of parties have developed since the beginning of the 19th century: conservative, liberal, and socialist. Each reflects the interests of a particular social class and expounds a particular political ideology. After World War I other categories of parties developed that were partly the result of divisions or transformations of older parties. Communist parties began as splinter groups of socialist parties, and Christian Democratic parties attempted to weld together moderate socialists and conservatives and some liberals. Other distinctive types of party emerged in some countries. In Scandinavia, liberal rural parties developed in the 19th century, reflecting a long tradition of separate representation of the rural population. In many countries ethnic minorities formed the basis of nationalist parties, which then either joined existing parties or divided them.

Second-round ballots being counted during 2011 local elections in Lyon, France. Second balloting gives small parties a chance to win elective seats and helps assure proportional representation within a multiparty system. © AP Images

The appearance of socialism in the 19th century upset the earlier lines of battle between conservatives and liberals and tended to throw the latter two groups into a common defense of capitalism. Logically, this situation should have led to the fusion of conservatives and liberals into one bourgeois party that would have presented a united stand against socialism. This is, in fact, what happened in Great Britain after World War I.

One of the most important factors determining the number of parties operating within a particular country is the electoral system. Proportional representation tends to favour the development of multiparty systems because it ensures representation in the legislature for even small parties. The majority, single-ballot system tends to produce a two-party system, because it excludes parties that may gain substantial numbers of votes but not the majority of votes necessary to elect a representative within a constituency. The majority system with a second ballot favours a multi-party system tempered by alliances between parties. Such a system is very rare, found only in the German Empire (1871–1914) and in the French Third and Fifth (since 1958) republics. Voters choose between the parties that did best in a first ballot. This leaves small parties at a disadvantage but, nevertheless, gives them opportunity to strengthen their role during the second balloting as long as they are willing to enter into alliances with the leading parties.

Another factor producing multiparty systems is the intensity of political conflicts. If, within a given political movement, extremists are numerous, then it is difficult for the moderates in that party to join with them in a united front. Two rival parties are likely to be formed. Thus, the power of the Jacobins among 19th-century French liberals contributed to the inability of the moderates to form one great liberal party, as was successfully achieved in Great Britain. Likewise, the power of the extremists among the conservatives was an obstacle to the development of a strong conservative party.

The distinction between the multiparty system and the two-party system corresponds largely to a distinction between two types of Western political regime. In a two-party situation the administration has, in effect, an assurance of a majority in the legislature, deriving from the predominance of one party; it has, therefore, a guarantee of continuance and effectiveness. Such a system is often referred to as majority parliamentarianism. In a multiparty situation, on the other hand, it is quite rare for one party to have a majority in the legislature. Governments must, therefore, be founded on coalitions, which are always more heterogeneous and more fragile than a single party. The result is less stability and less political power. Such systems may be referred to as nonmajority parliamentarianism.

In practice, majority and nonmajority parliamentary systems do not coincide exactly with two-party systems and multiparty systems. For, if each of the two parties is flexible and does not control the voting patterns of its members (as is the case in the United States), the numerical majority of one of the parties matters little. It can happen, moreover, that one party in a multiparty system will hold an absolute majority of seats in the legislature so that no coalition is required. Such a situation is unusual but did occur in West Germany, Italy, and Belgium at various times after 1945.

Ordinarily, however, a coalition will be the only means of attaining a parliamentary majority within the framework of the multiparty system. Coalitions are by nature more heterogeneous and more unstable than a grouping made up of one party, but their effectiveness varies greatly according to the discipline and organization of the parties involved. In the case of flexible parties that are undisciplined and that allow each legislator to vote on his own, the coalition will be weak and probably short-lived. The instability and weakness of governments is at its maximum in such situations, of which the Third French Republic provides a good example.

If, on the other hand, the parties involved in a coalition are rigid and disciplined, it is possible for a system quite similar to the two-party system to develop. This is often the case when two opposing alliances are formed, one on the left and one on the right, and when both are strong enough to endure through the legislative session. This type of coalition, referred to as bipolarized, introduces elements of the two-party system into a multiparty framework.

The system of bipolar alliances may be contrasted with the system of a centrist alliance. Rather than the parties on the right forming a centre-right coalition to oppose a centre-left coalition, there is the possibility that the centre-left and the centre-right will join forces and reject the extremes at both ends of the political spectrum. Such a situation occurred in Germany during the Weimar Republic, when the government rested on a majority formed of a coalition of Catholic Centrists and Social Democrats, with opposition coming from the communists and the nationalists on the extreme left and right.

Centrist coalitions all tend to give the average citizen a sense of political alienation. In rejecting both extremes, coalitions may well be isolating the radical, unstable elements, but the governing coalition may tend to be unresponsive to new ideas, uninspiringly pragmatic, and too ready to compromise. This situation gives rise to a more or less permanent breach between practical politics and political ideals. An advantage of bipolarization or of the two-party system is that the moderates of both sides must collaborate with those who are more extreme in their views, and the extremists must be willing to work with those who are more moderate. The pressure from the extremists prevents the moderates from getting bogged down, while collaboration with the moderates lends a touch of realism to the policies of the extremists.

TWO-PARTY SYSTEMS

A fundamental distinction must be made between the two-party system as it is found in the United States and as it is found in Great Britain. Although two major parties dominate political life in the two countries, the system operates in quite different ways.

THE AMERICAN TWO-PARTY SYSTEM

The United States has always had a two-party system, first in the opposition between the Federalists and the Anti-Federalists, then in the competition between the Republicans and the Democrats. There have been frequent third-party movements in the history of the country, but they have always failed. Presidential elections seem to have played an important role in the formation of this type of two-party system. The mechanism of a national election in so large a country has necessitated very large political organizations and, at the same time, relatively simplified choices for the voter.

American parties are different from their counterparts in other Western countries. They are not tied in the same way to the great social and ideological movements that have so influenced the development of political life in Europe during the last two centuries. There have been socialist parties at various times in the history of the United States, but they have never challenged the dominance of the two major parties. It can be argued that the main reason for the failure of socialist parties in America has been the high degree of upward mobility permitted by a rich and continually expanding economy. The consequence of this mobility has been that class consciousness has never developed in the United States in a manner that would encourage the formation of large socialist or communist parties.

In comparison with European political movements, therefore, American parties have appeared as two varieties of one liberal party, and within each party can be found a wide range of opinion, going from the right to the left.

The American parties have a flexible and decentralized structure, marked by the absence of discipline and rigid hierarchy. This was the structure of most of the cadre-type parties of the 19th century, a structure that most liberal parties have retained. Federalism and a concern for local autonomy accentuate the lack of rigid structure and the weakness of lines of authority in the parties. Organization may be relatively strong and homogeneous at the local level, but such control is much weaker on the state level and practically nonexistent on the national level. There is some truth to the observation that the United States has not two parties but 100—that is, two in each state. But it is also true that each party develops a certain degree of national unity for the presidential election and that the leadership of the president within his party gives the victorious party some cohesion.

In voting, Republicans and Democrats were usually found on both sides until about the first decade of the 21st century, when, for a variety of reasons, voting became increasingly partisan. Through the 20th century, alliances between liberal Republicans and Democrats against conservative Republicans and Democrats tended to develop. But neither bloc was stable, and the alignment varied from one vote to another. As a consequence, despite the existence of a two-party system, no stable legislative majority was possible. In order to have his budget adopted and his legislation passed, the president of the United States was forced to carefully gather the necessary votes on every question, bearing the wearisome task of constantly forming alliances. The American two-party system was thus a pseudo-two-party system, because each party provides only a loose framework within which shifting coalitions are formed.

THE BRITISH TWO-PARTY SYSTEM

Another form of the two-party system is operative in Great Britain and in New Zealand. The situation in Australia is affected somewhat by the presence of a third party, the Nationals (formerly [1982–2006] the National Party of Australia). A tight alliance between the Australian Liberal Party and the Nationals introduces, however, a rather rigid bipolarization with the Labour Party. The system thus tends to operate on a two-party basis. Canada also possesses what is essentially a two-party system, Liberals or Conservatives usually being able to form a working majority without the help of the small, regionally based parties.

Great Britain has had two successive two-party alignments: Conservative and Liberal prior to 1914 and Conservative and Labour since 1935. The period from 1920 to 1935 constituted an intermediate phase between the two. Britain's Conservative Party is actually a Conservative-Liberal Party, resulting from a fusion of the essential elements of the two great 19th-century parties. Despite the name Conservative, its ideology corresponds to political and economic liberalism. A similar observation could be made about the other major European conservative parties, such as the German Christian Democratic Party and the Belgian Social Christian Party.

The British two-party system depends on the existence of rigid parties—that is, parties in which there is effective discipline regarding parliamentary voting patterns. In every important vote, all party members are required to vote as a bloc and to follow to the letter the directives that they agreed upon collectively or that were decided for them by the party leaders. A relative flexibility may at times be tolerated, but only to the extent that such a policy does not compromise the action of the government. It may be admissible for some party members to abstain from voting if their abstention does not alter the results of the vote. Thus, the leader of the majority party (who is at the same time the prime minister) is likely to remain in power throughout the session of Parliament, and the legislation he or she proposes will likely be adopted. There is no longer any real separation of power between the executive and legislative branches, for the government and its parliamentary majority form a homogeneous and solid bloc before which the opposition has no power other than to make its criticisms known. During the four or five years for which a Parliament meets, the majority in power is completely in control, and only internal difficulties within the majority party can limit its power.

Since each party is made up of a disciplined group with a recognized leader who becomes prime minister if his or her party wins the legislative elections, these elections perform the function of selecting both the legislature and the government. In voting to make one of the party leaders the head of the government, the British assure the leader of a disciplined parliamentary majority. The result is a political system that is at once stable, democratic, and strong. Indeed, many would argue that it is more stable, more democratic, and stronger than systems anywhere else.

This situation presupposes that both parties are in agreement with regard to the fundamental rules of a democracy. If a fascist party and a communist party were opposed to each other in Great Britain, the two-party system would not last very long. The winner would zealously suppress the opponent and rule alone.

The system, of course, does have its weak points, especially insofar as it tends to frustrate the innovative elements within both parties. But it is possible that this situation is preferable to what would happen if the more extreme elements within the parties were permitted to engage in unrealistic policies. The risk of immobility is in fact a problem for any party in a modern industrial society, and not just for those in a two-party situation. The problem is related to the difficulties involved in creating new organizations capable of being taken seriously by an important segment of the population and in revitalizing long-standing organizations encumbered by established practices and entrenched interests.

SINGLE-PARTY SYSTEMS

There have been three historical forms of the single-party system: communist, fascist, and that found in developing countries. In communist countries of the 20th century, the party was considered to be the spearhead of the urban working class and of other workers united with it (e.g., peasants, intellectuals, and so on). Fascist development of single-party systems in a single-party state have never played as important a role as communist parties in an analogous situation.

THE COMMUNIST MODEL

In the 20th century, the role of the communist party was to aid in the building of a socialist regime during the transitory phase between capitalism and pure socialism, called the dictatorship of the proletariat. An understanding of the exact role of the party requires an appreciation of the Marxist conception of the evolution of the state. In countries based on private ownership of the means of production, the power of the state, according to the Marxist point of view, is used to further the interests of the controlling capitalists. In the first stage of revolution the power of the state is broken. Power, however, still has to be wielded to prevent counterrevolution and to facilitate the transition to communism, at which stage coercion will no longer be necessary. Thus, the party, in effect, assumes the coercive functions of the state during the dictatorship of the proletariat or, to be more accurate, during the dictatorship of the party in the name of the proletariat.

In all communist countries, the structure of the party was determined largely by the need for it to govern firmly while at the same time maintaining its contact with the masses of the people. Party members were a part of the general public, of which they were the most active and most politically conscious members. They remained in contact with the masses by means of a network of party cells that were present everywhere. Party leaders were thus always "listening in on the masses," and the masses were always informed of decisions of party leaders, as long as the communication network was working in both directions.

The party was not only a permanent means of contact between the people and party leaders but also a propaganda instrument. Political indoctrination was essential to the survival of communist parties, and many resources were devoted to it. Indoctrination was accomplished in training schools, by means of "education" campaigns, by censorship, and through the untiring efforts of militants, who played a role similar to that of the clergy in organized religion. The party was thus the guardian of orthodoxy and had the power to condemn and to excommunicate.

In the traditional communist model, the party hierarchy, then, and not the official state hierarchy, had the real power. The first secretary of the party was the most important figure of the regime, and, whether the party leadership was in the hands of one person or several, the party remained the centre of political power.

Near the end of the 20th century, however, the communist model began to change as the centre of power began shifting toward a popularly elected state hierarchy. A younger generation of communist leaders, openly critical of the party's inefficient, unresponsive, and domineering management of the government—particularly the economy—sought a return to Vladimir Ilich Lenin's original concepts of democratic centralism and socialism. In some countries, democratic concepts were emphasized, and constitutional amendments eliminated the party's official control, clearing the way for a multiparty system.

THE FASCIST MODEL

In Italy, the National Fascist Party was never the single most important element in the regime, and its influence was often secondary. In Spain the Falange never played a crucial role, and in Portugal the National Union was a very weak organization even at the height of dictator António Salazar's strength. Only in Germany did the National Socialist Party have a great influence on the state. But, in the end, Adolf Hitler's dictatorship was dependent on his private army, the SS (Schutzstaffel), which formed a separate element within the party and which was closed to outside influences, and on the Gestapo, which was a state organization and not an organization of the party. The fascist party in the single-party state had a policing or military function rather than an ideological one.

After their rise to power, the fascist parties in both Germany and Italy gradually ceased to perform the

GAMAL ABDEL NASSER

(b. Jan. 15, 1918,
Alexandria, Egypt—d.
Sept. 28, 1970, Cairo)

Gamal Abdel Nasser was
an Egyptian army officer
who served as prime minister (1954–56) and president
(1956–70) of Egypt. In his
youth, he took part in anti-
British demonstrations. As
an army officer, he led a coup
that deposed the royal family (1952) and installed Gen.
Muḥammad Naguib as head
of state. In 1954 he deposed
Naguib and made himself
prime minister. The Islamist
Muslim Brotherhood tried

*Gamal Abdel Nasser, photograph
by Yousuf Karsh.* © Karsh from
Rapho/Photo Researchers

to assassinate him but failed. In 1956 he promulgated a constitution that made Egypt a one-party socialist state with himself
as president. In the same year, he nationalized the Suez Canal
and secured Soviet assistance to build the Aswan High Dam
after the U.S. and Britain canceled their offer of aid. Soon there-
after, Egypt weathered an attack by British, French, and Israeli
forces. A charismatic figure, he succeeded briefly in forming
the United Arab Republic with Syria (1958–61). He led the Arab
world in the disastrous Six-Day War against Israel but had ten-
tatively accepted a U.S. peace plan for Egypt and Israel when
he died of a heart attack. He was succeeded by Anwar el-Sādāt.

function of maintaining contact between the people and the government, a function that is usually performed by the party in a single-party situation. It was possible to observe a tendency for the party to close in upon itself while suppressing its deviant members. The renewal of the party was then assured through recruitment from youth organizations, from which the most fanatical elements, the products of a gradual selection process starting at a very early age, entered the party. The party tended, therefore, to constitute a closed order.

SINGLE PARTIES IN DEVELOPING COUNTRIES

Some of the communist parties in power in developing countries did not differ significantly from their counterparts in industrialized countries. This is certainly true of the Vietnamese Communist Party and the Korean Workers' Party (North Korea). There have always been, however, countries in which the single party in power could not be characterized in terms of a traditional European counterpart. This observation applies to, for example, the former Arab Socialist Union in Egypt, the former Democratic Constitutional Rally in Tunisia, and the National Liberation Front in Algeria, as well as many other parties in sub-Saharan Africa.

Most of these parties claimed to be more or less socialist or at least progressive, while remaining far removed from communism and, in some cases, ardent foes of communism. Pres. Gamal Abdel Nasser attempted to establish a moderate and nationalistic socialism in Egypt. In Tunisia the Democratic Constitutional Rally was more republican than socialist and was inspired more by the example of the reforms in Turkey under Kemal Atatürk than by Nasserism. In sub-Saharan Africa, single parties often claimed to be socialist, but with few exceptions they rarely were in practice.

Single parties in developing countries have rarely been as well organized as were communist parties. In Turkey the Republican People's Party was more a cadre party than a mass-based party. In Egypt it was necessary to organize a core of professional politicians within the framework of a pseudoparty of the masses. In sub-Saharan Africa the parties were most often genuinely mass-based, but the membership appeared to be motivated primarily by personal attachment to the leader or by tribal loyalties, and organization was not usually very strong. It is this weakness in organization that explained the secondary role played by such parties in government.

Some regimes, however, endeavoured to develop the role of the party to the fullest extent possible. The politics of Atatürk in Turkey were an interesting case study in this regard. It was also Nasser's goal to increase the influence of the Arab Socialist Union, thereby making it the backbone of the regime. This process was significant in that it represented an attempt to move away from the traditional dictatorship, supported by the army or based on tribal traditions or on charismatic leadership, toward a modern dictatorship, supported by one political party. Single-party systems can institutionalize dictatorships by making them survive the life of one dominant figure.

THE FUTURE OF POLITICAL PARTIES

It has often been said in the West that political parties are in a state of decline. Actually, this has been a long-standing opinion in certain conservative circles, arising largely out of a latent hostility to parties, which are viewed as a divisive force among citizens, a threat to national unity, and an enticement to corruption and demagoguery. In certain European countries—France, for example—right-wing political organizations have even refused to call themselves parties, using instead such terms as "movement," "union," "federation," and "centre." And it cannot be denied that to some extent the major European and American parties of the late 20th and early 21st centuries do appear old and rigid in comparison with their condition at the turn of the 20th century or immediately following World War I.

In terms of size and number, however, political parties are not declining but growing. At the turn of the 20th century they were confined mainly to Europe and North America, and elsewhere they were quite weak or nonexistent. In the early 21st century, parties are found practically everywhere in the world. And in Europe and North America there are generally far more people holding membership in parties than prior to 1914. Parties of the early 21st century are larger, stronger, and better organized than those of the late 19th century. In the industrialized nations, especially in western Europe, parties have become less revolutionary and innovative, and this factor may explain the rigid and worn-out image that they sometimes present. But even this phenomenon is found only in a limited area and may, perhaps, pass.

The growth of parties into very large organizations may be responsible for the feelings of powerlessness on the part of many individuals who are involved in them. This is a problem experienced by people who find themselves part of any large organization, whether it be a political party, business enterprise, corporation, or union. The difficulties involved in reforming or changing political parties that have become large and institutionalized, coupled with the next-to-impossible task of creating new parties likely to reach sufficient strength to be taken seriously by the electorate, have resulted in much frustration and impatience with the party system. Such feelings contributed to the emergence of the right-wing Tea Party movement in the United States in 2009 and of the left-wing Occupy Wall Street movement in the U.S. and other countries in 2011. Nevertheless, it is difficult to imagine how democracy could function in a large industrialized country without political parties. In the modern world, democracy and political parties are two facets of the same reality, the inside and outside of the same fabric.

CHAPTER 2

Interest Groups

A n interest group is an association of individuals or organizations, usually formally organized, that, on the basis of one or more shared concerns, attempts to influence public policy. All interest groups share a desire to affect government policy to benefit themselves or their causes. Their goal could be a policy that exclusively benefits group members or one segment of society (e.g., government subsidies for farmers) or a policy that advances a broader public purpose (e.g., improving air quality). They attempt to achieve their goals by lobbying—that is, by attempting to bring pressure to bear on policy makers to gain policy outcomes in their favour.

Interest groups are a natural outgrowth of the communities of interest that exist in all societies, from narrow groups such as the Japan Eraser Manufacturers Association to broad groups such as the American Federation of Labor–Congress of Industrial Organizations (AFL-CIO) and to even broader organizations such as the military. Politics and interests are inseparable. Interests are a prevalent, permanent, and essential aspect of all political systems—democratic, authoritarian, and totalitarian regimes alike. Furthermore, interest groups exist at all levels of government—national, state, provincial, and local—and increasingly they have occupied an important role in international affairs.

The common goals and sources of interest groups obscure, however, the fact that they vary widely in their form and lobbying strategies both within and across political systems. This chapter provides a broad overview that explains these differences and the role that interest groups play in society.

THE NATURE OF INTEREST GROUPS

An interest group is usually a formally organized association that seeks to influence public policy. This broad definition, increasingly used by scholars, contrasts with older, narrower ones that include only private associations that have a distinct, formal organization, such as Italy's Confindustria (General Confederation of Industry), the United States's National Education Association, and Guatemala's Mutual Support Group (human rights organization). One problem with such a narrow definition is

A 1995 rally in Guatemala organized by the human rights support group GAM. Private associations such as GAM represent just one type of modern-day special interest group. Macarthur McBurney/ AFP/Getty Images

that many formally organized entities are not private. The most important lobbying forces in any society are the various entities of government: national, regional, and local government agencies and institutions such as the military.

Another reason to opt for a broad definition is that in all societies there are many informal groups that are, in effect, interest groups but would not be covered by the narrower definition. For example, in all political systems there are influential groups of political and professional elites that may not be recognized as formal groups but are nonetheless crucial in informally influencing public policy.

Some interest groups consist of individuals such as ranchers or fruit growers who may form farm commodity organizations. In other instances, an interest group consists not of individuals but of organizations or businesses, such as the Histadrut (General Federation of Labour) in Israel and Oxfam International, a federation of 12 national organizations that provides relief and development aid to impoverished or disaster-stricken communities worldwide. These types of organizations are called peak associations, as they are, in effect, the major groups in their area of interest in a country.

The term *interest* rather than *interest group* is often used to denote broad or less-formalized political constituencies, such as the agricultural interest and the environmental interest—segments of society that may include many formal interest groups. Similarly, *interest* is often used when considering government entities working to influence other governments (e.g., a local government seeking to secure funding from the national government). In authoritarian and developing societies, where formal interest groups are restricted or not as well developed, *interest* is often used to designate broader groupings such as government elites and tribal leaders.

TYPES OF INTEREST GROUPS

Interests and interest groups in all types of political systems can be placed broadly in five categories: (1) economic interests, (2) cause groups, (3) public interests, (4) private and public institutional interests, and (5) nonassociational groups and interests.

Economic interest groups are ubiquitous and the most prominent in all countries. There are literally thousands of them with offices in national capitals from London to Ottawa to New Delhi to Canberra. There are several different kinds of economic interests: business groups (e.g., the Canadian Federation of Independent Business, the Confederation of British Industry, and Nestlé SA, headquartered in Switzerland and with operations throughout the world), labour groups (e.g., IG Metall in Germany, the Trades Union Congress in the United Kingdom, and the AFL-CIO in the United States), farm groups (e.g., the Irish Farmers' Association in the republic of Ireland and the American Farm Bureau Federation), and professional groups (e.g., the American Bar Association and the Czech Medical Chamber).

Cause groups are those that represent a segment of society but whose primary purpose is noneconomic and usually focused on promoting a particular cause or value. This category is wide-ranging, including churches and religious organizations (e.g., Catholic Action in Italy), veterans' groups (e.g., the Union Française des Associations d'Anciens Combattants et Victimes de Guerre [French Union of Associations of Combatants and Victims of War]), and groups supporting the rights of people with disabilities (e.g., the Spanish National Organisation for the Blind [ONCE] and Autism Speaks in the United States). Some cause groups are single-issue groups, focusing very narrowly on their issue to the exclusion of all others — such

TRADE ASSOCIATION

A trade association (also called a trade organization), is a voluntary association of business firms organized on a geographic or industrial basis to promote and develop commercial and industrial opportunities within its sphere of operation, to voice publicly the views of members on matters of common interest, or in some cases to exercise some measure of control over prices, output, and channels of distribution.

The oldest and most widespread trade associations are chambers of commerce, also known as commercial associations, boards of trade, and development associations. Although in most countries their focus is the development of business opportunity and community improvement, in France the chambers of commerce have served as agencies of official administrative control of public commercial institutions. In 1599 the city of Marseille established the first *chambre de commerce* and empowered it to send consuls, embassies, and commercial missions to certain countries. Modern French *chambres* have owned and administered sections of stock exchanges, bonded warehouses, public salesrooms, and port, dock, inland waterway, and airfield facilities.

The first British chamber of commerce—a voluntary association of independent firms in industry, commerce, and trade—was organized in 1768 in Jersey, Channel Islands, to protect and promote common local interests. Many new chambers were formed both in Britain and abroad as economic development went forward—e.g., in New York state in 1768, in Calcutta (Kolkata) in 1834, and in Paris in 1873. Today many countries have chambers of commerce abroad, in important cities throughout the world.

The one organization truly international in scope is the International Chamber of Commerce, a world federation of business organizations, business firms, and business leaders founded in 1920.

Trade associations organized according to industries or products have a significant impact on prices, sales, output, and technology, although they rarely extend their activities beyond national boundaries. In their modern form these associations began in the late 19th century in many countries, including the United States, Britain, and Japan, but they existed as early as 1821 in France. Most trade associations confine themselves to voicing their members' views on matters of common interest. Particularly in the United States, this exercise has included legislative lobbying and campaign contributions. In some countries they may also have some control over prices and production levels, but in those countries with strong antitrust legislation (e.g., the United States) this type of organization has been short-lived.

Separate employers' organizations have been founded in some countries, including Britain, Australia, and India, to deal with labour questions. French industrial federations, on the other hand, represent the interests of the members both as manufacturers and as employers.

as those favouring or opposing abortion rights or foxhunting—though most cause groups are more broadly based.

Whereas economic interests and most cause groups benefit a narrow constituency, public interest groups promote issues of general public concern (e.g., environmental protection, human rights, and consumer rights). Many public interest groups operate in a single country (e.g., the Federal Association of Citizen-Action Groups for Environmental Protection in Germany). Others, such as the Sierra Club, which has chapters in the United States and Canada, may operate in only a few countries. Increasingly, however, many public interest groups have a much broader international presence, with activities in many countries (e.g., Amnesty International and the International Campaign to Ban Landmines).

Private and public institutional interests constitute another important category. These are not membership groups (hence, they are termed *interests* as opposed to *interest groups*) but private organizations such as businesses or public entities such as government departments. However, like interest groups, they attempt to affect public policy in their favour. Private institutional interests include think tanks such as the Brookings Institution in the United States and the Adam Smith Institute in the United Kingdom; private universities; and various forms of news media, particularly newspapers, that advocate on behalf of a particular issue or philosophy. But by far the largest component of this category is government in its many forms. At the national level, government agencies, such as the British Department for Environment, Food and Rural Affairs, lobby on their own behalf to secure funding or to prioritize certain issues. At the regional level, public universities lobby the appropriate government (e.g., provincial governments in Canada and state governments in the United States) for funding or legislation that benefits them. At the local level, school boards may lobby the local government for money for a new school gymnasium or for more funding for educational programs. At the international level, the United Nations may lobby its members to pay their outstanding dues to the organization or to carry out Security Council resolutions.

Governmental institutional interests are often the most important interests in authoritarian regimes, where private interest groups are severely restricted or banned. In communist countries (both before and since the fall of the Soviet Union and its satellites in eastern Europe), such governmental interests have included economic planning and agricultural agencies and the secret police. In some

Occupy Wall Street protestors march in New York City. Begun in September 2011 as a local protest against corporate greed, the Occupy movement quickly spread to more than 100 cities around the world. Mario Tama/Getty Images

Muslim countries (e.g., Iran and Saudi Arabia), religious institutions are prominent interests.

Although formally organized associations play a predominant role in traditional lobbying efforts, non-associational groups and interests often have an important influence. Such interests lack a formal organization or permanent structure. They include spontaneous protest movements formed in reaction to a particular policy or event and informal groups of citizens and officials of public or private organizations. For example, French farmers have sometimes held up traffic in Paris to protest government agricultural policy, and protesters have mounted demonstrations against the power of corporations, as did the Occupy Wall Street movement in 2011.

Political systems at different levels of development and with different types of regimes manifest different combinations and varying ranges of these five types of interest groups. In western Europe, Canada, the United States, and Japan, for example, each of the five types of interests are represented in large numbers and have developed sophisticated strategies and tactics. In developing countries and in those with authoritarian regimes, there is a much narrower range of economic groups, very few (if any) public interest and cause groups, and some government interests. In these regimes, informal interests are generally the most important and the most numerous.

COMMON CHARACTERISTICS OF INTEREST GROUPS

Most interest groups are not formed for political purposes. They usually develop to promote programs and disseminate information to enhance the professional, business, social, or avocational interests of their members. Much of this activity is nonpolitical, as when the

American Association of University Professors (AAUP) provides low-cost life insurance for its members or when the American Automobile Association negotiates discounts with service providers for its members. But many such interest groups enter the political arena when they believe there is no other way to protect their interests or because they want to secure government funding.

In their nonpolitical role, interest groups may have several functions, but, when they become enmeshed in the political sphere, they have one overriding goal: to gain favourable outcomes from public policy decisions. In the political realm, interest groups perform important functions, particularly in a democracy but also in an authoritarian regime. These include aggregating and representing the interests of groups of individuals in a way that a single individual would not be able to do, helping to facilitate government by providing policy makers with information that is essential to making laws, and educating their members on issues and perhaps giving them political experience for entering politics. In addition to providing this political experience, groups sometimes actively recruit candidates for public office, with the hope that once elected these individuals will support their cause.

Interest groups in most democracies are also a source of financial support for election campaigns. In the United States the development of political action committees (PACs) after World War II was geared to providing money to candidates running for public office. In western Europe, campaign funding is provided by many interest groups, particularly trade unions for social democratic parties as in Sweden and Germany. Mass parties in authoritarian regimes also often rely on interest groups for support. For example, in Argentina Juan Perón used the General Confederation of Labour (CGT), the trade union peak association, to gain and maintain the presidency

Thousands of Argentinean laborers gather around the image of former president Juan Perón in 2009. Trade unions formed the base of Perón's support during his presidency. Daniel Garcia/ AFP/Getty Images

POLITICAL ACTION COMMITTEE

Political action committees (PACs) are organizations in the United States whose purpose is to raise and distribute campaign funds to candidates seeking political office. PACs are generally formed by corporations, labour unions, trade associations, or other organizations or individuals. They channel the voluntary contributions they raise primarily to candidates for elective offices in the U.S. House of Representatives and the U.S. Senate. PACs may also spend their funds on what are termed independent expenditures—defined in law as a message "expressly advocating the election or defeat of a clearly identified candidate that is not made in cooperation, consultation, or concert with, or at the request or suggestion of, a candidate, a candidate's authorized committee, or their agents, or a political party or its agents."

The first PAC was created in 1944 by the Congress of Industrial Organizations, which sought to raise funds to assist the reelection of Pres. Franklin D. Roosevelt. PACs were an ancillary part of political campaigns in the United States until the Federal Election Campaign Act of 1971 (and its amendment in 1974). Ostensibly, the law was established to reduce the influence of money in campaigns by setting strict limits on the amount a particular corporation, union, or private individual could give to a candidate. By soliciting smaller contributions from a much larger number of individuals, however, PACs were able to circumvent these limitations and provide substantial funds for candidates. Following the reforms, the number of PACs proliferated, from about 600 in the early 1970s to more than 4,000 by 2010. With this proliferation came a massive escalation in the cost of running for federal office in the United States.

While most PACs have historically been associated with businesses or unions, in the early 21st century new kinds of PACs began to exert greater influence. Among them are Leadership PACs, which are often formed by politicians who might aspire to higher office (particularly the presidency) or more influence within their political party by raising funds and disbursing them to the campaigns of other candidates; Super PACs, which were established in 2010 following the U.S. Supreme Court's *Citizens United* v. F*ederal Election Commission* decision (and the subsequent *SpeechNow.org* v. *Federal Election Commission* ruling) and which allow both corporations and unions to make independent expenditures from their general treasuries; and nonconnected PACs, which are independent of corporations, unions, and political parties and which make contributions and expenditures to support a particular ideology or issue.

of that country from 1946 to 1955. In addition to financial resources, members of interest groups are important resources for grassroots campaigning, such as operating telephone banks to call prospective voters, canvassing neighbourhoods door-to-door, and organizing get-out-the-vote efforts on election day.

FACTORS SHAPING INTEREST GROUPS

Various factors shape the environment in which interest groups operate and provide a foundation for understanding similarities and differences in types of interest groups around the world.

The level of socioeconomic development within a society usually can inform observers about how highly developed and represented society's interests are. In more economically prosperous societies, the number of interest groups and the people belonging to them is usually quite extensive. By contrast, in less affluent countries, the number of interest groups is usually quite limited, and their level of sophistication is usually lower. In democracies, lobbying is more formalized and wide-ranging than in authoritarian and developing countries, where it is largely informal, with only a small segment of society having access to government.

In democratic systems, interest groups are generally free to operate, though the acceptance of the scope of their activity by the general public and politicians may vary. Even in democracies, many may consider interest groups detrimental to the operation of society and government. (In general, however, there is a broad consensus in most democracies that interest groups play a vital and necessary role in political and economic life.) In postcommunist Lithuania, for example, there was skepticism of interest groups both among the public (a hangover of the fear of belonging to banned groups in the former communist regime) and among some politicians who believed such groups acted as an impediment in the transition to democracy by promoting their special interests over that of society. In contrast to democracies, authoritarian regimes often restrict and may even ban group formation and lobbying.

A country's political culture—the characteristic shared values of the citizens upon which government is based and upon which certain political activities are considered acceptable or not—varies from country to country. In all political systems, be they democratic or authoritarian, the ideological underpinnings of society influence the pattern of interest-group involvement in the political process— including, potentially, their exclusion from the process entirely. In Sweden, for example, where there exists a broad social democratic consensus that believes all interests should be taken into account in the policy-making process, the government actually organizes and funds groups (e.g., immigrant workers) that might not form otherwise. In contrast, the official ideology of communist regimes did not generally officially recognize the rights of interests to organize. Thus, they tended to operate unofficially and were subject to potential legal action by the government.

The location of political power in the political system determines the access points and methods of influence used by interest groups. In authoritarian regimes, power usually lies with the dictator or a small cadre of officials. Thus, any interest-group activity in such systems will be narrowly directed at these officials. In democracies, power is more diffused. In parliamentary systems, such as Canada and New Zealand, the executive is chosen from the legislature, and, because of party discipline, power tends to be concentrated in the executive, which therefore becomes the focus of lobbying. In presidential systems, particularly the United States, where there is a separation of powers between the executive and legislative branches, a lobbying strategy must focus on both branches of government.

Australian prime minister Kevin Rudd (left) meets with former U.S. vice president and current environmental lobbyist Al Gore in 2009. Special interest groups lobby at all levels within federal systems of government. Newspix/Getty Images

In addition, in some countries, power is divided among multiple layers of government. In unitary systems, where central government is the locus of policy making, lobbying efforts can concentrate on that level of government. By contrast, in federal systems (e.g., the United States, Australia, and Germany), interest groups often find it necessary to mount simultaneous campaigns at both the national and state levels.

Which party or party coalition controls the government influences the relative importance and impact of interest groups within society. For example, in a democracy, if a left or centre-left government is in office, it is most likely that allied groups (e.g., labour unions and environmental groups) would have more influence on and be consulted more often by the government, whereas business groups usually have wider access and importance when a conservative government is in office. Even in authoritarian regimes, changes in the executive can bring about the increased success of some groups at the expense of others. For example, the shift from a civilian to a military dictatorship or vice versa in a host of African, Asian, and Latin American countries in the period from the 1930s to the 1980s changed the configuration of interest groups and interest-group influence.

INTEREST GROUPS AND PUBLIC POLICY

Two theories have been put forward to explain interest groups' influence on public policy: pluralism and neo-corporatism.

PLURALISM

Pluralists argue that the most realistic description of politics and policy making is a marketplace with more or less perfect competition. In theory, in this political marketplace many (or plural) perspectives—as represented by individuals, political parties, and interest groups and interests—compete to have their views heard by government and their favoured policies enacted. According to this conception, because of competition between the varied and diverse interests, no single interest is likely to have its views win consistently over others. The United States is invariably cited by scholars as the country coming closest to this model in practice, though other democracies also qualify, particularly those in the Anglo-American tradition such as Canada and Australia.

In practice, however, pluralism is often less than an ideal system of representation for achieving policy changes. First, different groups have different resources; some interests, such as those representing businesses or

Medical students gather on the steps of the U.S. Capitol before lobbying members of Congress in 2011. Doctors are among the more successful lobbyists because of the services they provide.
Tom Williams/CQ-Roll Call Group/Getty Images

affluent professions, are well-organized and well-financed, while others, such as those for the poor or for immigrant workers, are not. Such disparities may serve to tilt the balance of policy influence in favour of better-organized and better-financed groups. Second, the government is rarely neutral in the conflict-resolution process; it often favours some groups over others because it depends on them. For example, a government may rely on a major industry (e.g., tourism) or a particular service, such as that provided by doctors, and so these interests will have more sway over that government than those it does not rely upon (e.g., welfare recipients or groups for the arts).

These concerns have led to modifications of the pluralist model. An elitist perspective, such as that advanced by American political scientist Theodore Lowi, considers groups, interests, and individuals that are well-connected to government policy makers and well-financed as prime movers in interest-group activity and policy making. The advantage of such elites is enhanced in many Western democracies because of the advent of hyperpluralism—a development of the late 20th century, particularly in the United States. As so many groups have entered the lobbying game, the competition for the attention of policy makers has become intense, and those groups with resources and connections—the elite groups—have an advantage in the fight to be heard by policy makers.

NEO-CORPORATISM

Neo-corporatism is a much more structured theory of interest-group activity than pluralism. It is a modern version of state corporatism, which emerged in the late 19th century in authoritarian systems and had several manifestations in the first half of the 20th century—for example, in Adolf Hitler's Germany and Francisco Franco's Spain.

In this system, society is seen as a corporate—that is, united and hierarchical—body in which the government dominates and all sectors of society (e.g., business, the military, and labour) are required to work for the public interest as defined by the government.

Whereas state corporatism is coercive, neo-corporatism is, in theory, based on voluntary agreement between government and labour and business interests. The goal is primarily economic: the neo-corporatist model focuses on keeping costs and inflation in check so that the country can be competitive in international trade and maintain and enhance the domestic standard of living. To be able to establish and maintain a neo-corporatist interest-group system, a country has to have peak associations that are able to enforce the agreements between business, labour, and the government. Consequently, in Scandinavia, Germany, Austria, and Switzerland, for example, where there are major peak associations that dominate their respective economic sectors, neo-corporatism can best explain major interest-group activity.

Neo-corporatist theory also has its critics. Some argue that it is not a distinct interest-group system at all but rather just another form of pluralism. This is because it still functions within a pluralist political environment and only major groups are involved in this special relationship with government. All other groups and interests compete in the same way that they would in a pluralist system such as the United States. In addition, critics also claim that neo-corporatism is so varied in actual practice as to lack distinct core characteristics. The Scandinavian countries are highly neo-corporatist, but countries such as France and Belgium are much less so, and the form of neo-corporatism practiced in Japan does not incorporate labour. Similar to pluralism, neo-corporatism operates differently in different countries depending on sociopolitical and historical circumstances. In fact, it is best to understand the interest-group system in democratic countries as existing along a scale, with highly pluralist countries such as the United States (with no dominant peak associations) at one end, countries such as New Zealand, which combines elements of pluralism and neo-corporatism, in the middle, and predominantly neo-corporatist systems, such as those of Scandinavia, at the other end of the scale.

Theories of interest-group activity in non-pluralist regimes are less all-embracing because of the wide variety of such regimes. State corporatism helps explain group activity in some countries (e.g., Cuba). In former communist countries (e.g., those in eastern Europe), the leaders of groups were simply tools of the party elite. And in authoritarian countries in the developing world (e.g., the monarchies of Saudi Arabia and Tonga), it is the elite cliques close to the royal family that hold the most sway.

LOBBYING STRATEGIES AND TACTICS

Lobbying involves working to bring pressure to bear on policy makers to gain favourable policy outcomes. In order to accomplish their goals, interest groups develop a strategy or plan of action and execute it through specific tactics. The particular strategies developed and the specific tactics used, however, vary widely both among and within political systems.

Three factors are of particular importance in shaping lobbying strategies and tactics. One is whether the political system is democratic or authoritarian. Because there generally are few restrictions on interest groups in democratic societies, they have more options available (e.g., hiring lobbyists, using the press, and staging public demonstrations). Thus, strategies and tactics are more formalized and open than in authoritarian societies, where they must be more ad hoc and less publicly visible.

A second factor is the structure of the policy process. In democratic parliamentary systems, where the executive is drawn from the major political party or party coalition in the parliament (e.g., Finland, India, and the republic of Ireland), the legislative branch is less important than the prime minister and the cabinet in policy making. In contrast, because of the power placed in the U.S. Congress and state legislatures, the United States is one of the few countries in which legislative lobbying is a major strategy of interest groups. The courts in most parliamentary systems also play a minor role in policy making. Again, in contrast, in the United States the separation-of-powers system has provided the courts, which have the power to invalidate legislation, with a major role in policy making, and, as a result, litigation strategies are often vital to American interest groups.

A lobbyist for the environmental group Oceana, dressed as a fish, catching the attention of congressional staff members in 2007. Unconventional lobbying tactics are more acceptable in the U.S. than elsewhere. Tom Williams/CQ-Roll Call Group/Getty Images

A third factor is political culture as it relates to group activity and lobbying. In the United States, for example, the use of contract lobbyists—those hired by contract specifically to lobby government—is much more accepted than in most other Western democracies, including those of the European Union, where public officials usually prefer to deal directly with the members of the concerned group, organization, or business.

Three major factors can also be identified to explain why lobbying strategies and tactics vary within a political system. One is the nature of the group and its resources. "Insider" groups—those older and more traditional business, labour, and professional groups with extensive resources, including money and established access to public officials—are better able to pursue "insider tactics," utilizing their close friends and associates in government to promote their goals, and generally have many more options available to them than do "outsider" groups. Such outsider groups tend to be newer and sometimes promote radical causes. They usually lack key contacts with policy makers and major financial resources, and they often focus their energy on grassroots efforts, which may include letter writing or Internet campaigns or public demonstrations to gain media coverage (insider groups may also use such methods).

Second, whether the purpose is to promote or defeat a legislative proposal helps to explain variations in strategies and tactics across different political systems. For instance, in the United States, a system that was designed by its founders to prevent government action, the so-called "advantage of the defense," operates. All an interest has to do to stop a proposal is to get a sympathetic committee chair in the legislature to oppose it or a president or governor to veto it. To get a proposal enacted requires that it clear hurdles in both houses of the legislature and be signed by the executive. In contrast, in parliamentary

systems, with power concentrated in an executive committed to the platform of the major party or party coalition in
parliament, it is much harder to defeat something if it has
been agreed upon by the party beforehand.

Third, a country's political climate influences strategies taken by interest groups. Which party is in power
(such as one favourably disposed to an interest group's
agenda), the major issues facing the government, and the
country's budget circumstances will influence the types of
strategies an interest group uses. For example, the National
Education Association (NEA) in the United States pur-
sues a different strategy when Republicans are in power in
Washington, D.C., and in the states than when Democrats
are in power. The NEA has "insider status" with the
Democrats but generally not with the Republicans.

Although strategies and tactics vary between and within
political systems, there is one aspect of lobbying common
in all systems, whether democratic or authoritarian: building personal contacts between group representatives and
public officials to foster trust and credibility, and persuade
the government that it needs the group. In democracies,
tactics are usually broad-ranging, but building relationships
is universal regardless of the type of democratic system.
In authoritarian and developing political systems, personal contacts between political elites within and outside
of government are often the major tactic (and sometimes
the only tactic available). For example, patron-client networks, which are modern manifestations of court cliques
in traditional monarchies, are based not on a shared interest (as set out in the definition of an interest group) but on
the personal benefit of the patron and clients. However,
patron-client connections can work to represent and gain
benefits for a group, such as merchants or landowners.

Among democracies, it is in the United States that
interest-group activity is most accepted and displays the

widest range of tactics. The lobbying profession, both at the federal and the state level (and increasingly at the local level), is highly developed. In regard to lobbyists in Washington, D.C., in newspapers and other popular writings, they are often talked about in connection with the terms "K Street" and "Gucci gulch," as it is on K Street that many of the contract lobbying firms are located, and the corridors in the Capitol where lobbyists congregate have been nicknamed for the expensive shoes and garments they often wear. Increasingly, however, American-style tactics have been adopted in other democracies and in transitional systems. In the United Kingdom and other countries of the European Union, Australia, and Canada, lobbyists are becoming increasingly important (they are usually known by other designations, such as political consultants or government-affairs or public-affairs representatives), and there also has been more use of the media and increased campaign contributions.

INFLUENCE OF INTEREST GROUPS

Research conducted in the United States provides major insights into the factors that determine interest-group influence. Money is important in explaining the influence (or lack thereof) of interest groups, but, contrary to what might be believed by the public, it is not simply money that determines political clout. Factors determining the influence of individual interest groups include the group's financial resources, the managerial and political skills of its leaders, the size and cohesiveness of its membership, and political timing—presenting an issue when the political climate is right. Three factors appear to be of particular importance:

- How much influence a group has depends on the extent to which government officials need the group.

The more elected or appointed public officials rely on an interest, business, or organization, the greater its leverage will be over government. Some corporations may have a presence in many districts throughout the country, and decisions that affect them will affect employment in those districts, thus making it likely that members of the legislature from those districts will be favourably predisposed to legislation that the group supports. Moreover, many interest groups provide major financial backing to political campaigns. The more widely dispersed its funds are in a country, state, or local jurisdiction, the more likely that legislators will listen to the concerns of that group.

- Lobbyist–policy-maker relations are also important in explaining the relative power of an interest group, since it is at this point that the demands of the group are conveyed to government. The more skillful the lobbyists are in forging personal contact with government officials, the more successful the group is likely to be. As noted earlier, this is the case in both democratic and authoritarian systems alike. In the United States, political scientists have identified phenomena known as "iron triangles" and "policy niches" in regard to lobbyist–policy-maker relations. In such cases, lobbyists, members of the legislature, and, in particular, members of the key committees work together to get policy enacted. These arrangements typify a form of elitism with privileged access leading to established lobbyist–policy-maker relationships that gives "insiders" an upper hand in influencing public policy.
- The relative level of organized opposition to a group is essential to understanding the success or failure of that group. The more intense the opposition to a group's cause, the more difficult it will be to achieve its goals. Some groups have natural political enemies

(e.g., environmentalists versus developers and corporations versus labour unions). Other interests, such as those advocating stricter laws against domestic violence and child abuse, have little opposition, though such groups may be limited by the other factors that determine influence, such as a lack of financial resources.

INTEREST GROUPS IN INTERNATIONAL POLITICS

Interest groups have long been active in international affairs, but the level of that activity has increased significantly since World War II and particularly since the late 1960s. A confluence of factors accounts for the explosion in international lobbying activities. These include:

- the increasing importance of international organizations, such as the United Nations (UN) and its various agencies, and regional organizations, such as the European Union (EU), with jurisdictions that extend beyond national borders;
- the fact that many issues (e.g., environmental protection, wildlife management, and the fight against the child prostitution trade) require an international approach; and
- increasing awareness of issues because of advances in communications and the adoption of many international causes in Western democracies (where most international interests originate and operate) by an increasingly affluent middle class.

According to American political scientist Howard Tolley, an authority on international interest groups, without political parties and elections to voice concerns at the

U.S. president Barack Obama speaking at the 2011 Asia-Pacific Economic Cooperation (APEC) summit. International lobbying activity grew as organizations such as APEC adopted a more important role on the world political stage after World War II. Kevork Djansezian/Getty Images

international level, nongovernmental pressure groups are even more vital in world politics than interest groups are at the domestic level.

There are thousands of international lobbies, but four broad categories constitute the vast majority.

- Foreign governments and international organizations. Countries maintain a wide array of embassies and consulates in foreign countries, and they often use these and hired lobbyists to work for such benefits as foreign aid and military support, as well as to boost the country's image abroad. International organizations (e.g., UNESCO, Asia-Pacific Economic Cooperation, the Arab League, and the Organization of American States) use their resources in manners similar to governments.

- Multinational corporations (e.g., McDonald's, Coca Cola, Honda, and Procter & Gamble) and business trade associations (e.g., the International Chamber of Commerce). These often have extensive global or regional reach. Their major concerns in lobbying relate to issues similar to those that they have within individual countries and include ensuring favourable labour codes and tax structures, making trade as free as possible, ensuring favourable laws regarding government regulation of their product (e.g., food and drink) or service (e.g., telecommunications), and trying to minimize added costs such as those involving environmental regulations. Because of their extensive resources and the fact that the government relies on the economic advantages provided by these multinational corporations, they are often successful in achieving their lobbying goals.
- Special-interest and cause groups. These include the World Council of Churches, the Baptist World Alliance, the Anglican Communion, international networks of gay-rights groups, and the Inuit Circumpolar Council, an organization of indigenous peoples of the Arctic and subarctic regions of North America, Europe, and Asia. Such groups and organizations are involved in international lobbying for a variety of reasons and with mixed success. Some, such as churches, often lobby simply for the right to operate in a country and on behalf of human and civil rights and the poor. Others, such as indigenous groups, lobby for the rights of their compatriots with respect to preserving their customs and language and repatriating artifacts that may have been taken to other countries and are now housed in museums around the world (particularly in countries that were former colonizers).

- International public-interest groups (nongovernmental organizations [NGOs]). NGOs embrace a wide range of groups that focus on issues of broad public concern, such as human rights, child welfare, and the status of women, as opposed to the specific interests of particular businesses or sectors of society, such as automobile manufacturers and physicians. At the meeting in 1945 in San Francisco that drew up the UN charter, some 1,200 NGOs were in attendance. Though there is no current, reliable count of NGOs, they mushroomed in the period after World War II and numbered as many as 10,000 in the early 21st century. During the same period it was estimated that there were some 2,000 NGOs in Latin America alone. Significant among the multitude of NGOs operating in world politics today are Human Rights Watch, Oxfam International, CARE, Greenpeace, the World Wildlife Fund, Earth First!, and the Women's International League for Peace and Freedom. NGOs enjoy mixed success in their political activities, partly because governments rarely rely on these groups to maintain themselves in office. Most operate far from public view, and their successes may receive little publicity. Some, however, such as Greenpeace, receive major publicity for their campaigns.

THE REGULATION OF INTEREST GROUPS

Even though interest groups are indispensable to the operation of government in both democracies and authoritarian systems, they have the potential to promote the interests of a small segment of society at the expense of society as a whole. Consequently, there is criticism of interest-group activity in both democracies and authoritarian regimes. However, views of the negative effects of interest groups and ways of attempting to deal with them are different in democracies and authoritarian systems.

In pluralist systems there is a great degree of concern with how interest groups might undermine democracy. Groups in such systems often claim to pursue an agenda that is "in the public interest," but in practice they often serve rather narrow interests. In non-pluralist systems it is sometimes feared that interest groups will undermine the national interest or major government plans and commitments that are often expressed by a country's official ideology or through the statements of national officials.

To deal with potential problems of interest-group activity, many democratic governments and all authoritarian regimes adopt some form of regulation (control in authoritarian systems) of interest groups. In all systems, the goal of regulation is to promote the public interest, however defined, over that of the narrow segments of society represented by interest groups. In its specific form, however, regulation varies considerably in scope, focus, and form between democratic and authoritarian regimes.

Regulations in authoritarian systems are usually quite wide-ranging and are focused on controlling group formation and channeling the modes of activity that groups can pursue. In such systems, activity by particular interest groups may be prohibited (e.g., in communist systems in eastern Europe during the Cold War, nearly all private associations were banned), or groups may be allowed to form and participate but be co-opted and have their activities heavily circumscribed by the government.

In democracies the underlying principle of the regulation of interest groups is that it enhances democracy. However, few, if any, restrictions are placed on group formation and the right to lobby government. Indeed, these are rights guaranteed in many national constitutions. Instead, democracies attempt to address perceived ethical questions surrounding lobbying, such as a normative desire to create a somewhat-level playing field for groups in terms of access and influence. Most often this is attempted through public disclosure or the monitoring of interest-group activity by requiring interest groups and their lobbyists to register with public authorities and to declare their objects of lobbying as well as their income and expenditures. Even so, the extent of regulation varies widely across democracies. The United States has a long history of fairly extensive regulation, whereas the countries of western Europe generally have far less regulation. Australia attempted to implement a system of regulation in the early 1980s but abandoned it in the mid-1990s in favour of self-regulation by interest groups and lobbyists.

THE FUTURE OF INTEREST GROUPS

Interest groups will always be part of the political process. Moreover, their activity should increase in all future political systems for two reasons. First, government activity is likely to expand and affect existing interests more extensively and new interests in various ways, thereby forcing individuals and organizations to become politically active to protect or promote their interests. Second, globalization will likely increase international interest-group activity and result in an increasing interdependence between many domestic and international interests. This expansion, and particularly the internationalization of interest-group activity, will produce some homogenization in the organization of interests and the techniques they use to gain access and exert influence. However, specific governmental structures, political culture, deep-rooted ideology, historical practice, and short-term political circumstances will likely always work to give interest-group activity many unique elements in each country.

Public opinion is an aggregate of the individual views, attitudes, and beliefs, expressed by a significant proportion of a community. Some scholars treat the aggregate as a synthesis of the views of all or a certain segment of society, while others regard it as a collection of many differing or opposing views. Writing in 1918, the American sociologist Charles Horton Cooley emphasized public opinion as a process of interaction and mutual influence rather than a state of broad agreement. The American political scientist V.O. Key, Jr., defined public opinion in 1961 as "opinions held by private persons which governments find it prudent to heed." Subsequent advances in statistical and demographic analysis led by the 1990s to an understanding of public opinion as the collective view of a defined population, such as a particular demographic or ethnic group.

The influence of public opinion is not restricted to politics and elections. It is a powerful force in many other spheres, such as culture, fashion, literature and the arts, consumer spending, and marketing and public relations.

THEORETICAL AND PRACTICAL CONCEPTIONS

In his eponymous treatise on public opinion published in 1922, the American editorialist Walter Lippmann qualified his observation that democracies tend to make a mystery out of public opinion with the declaration that "there have

V.O. KEY, JR.

(b. March 13, 1908, Austin, Texas, U.S.—d. Oct. 4, 1963, Cambridge, Mass.)

Valdimer Orlando Key, Jr., was a U.S. political scientist who was known for his studies of the U.S. political process and for his contributions to the development of a more empirical and behavioral political science.

Educated at the University of Texas (B.A., 1929; M.A., 1930) and the University of Chicago (Ph.D., 1934), Key joined the faculty of the University of California at Los Angeles. In 1936–38 he served with the Social Science Research Council and the National Resources Planning Board. He taught at Johns Hopkins University (1938–49) with interruptions for government service with the Bureau of the Budget during World War II. He taught at Yale in 1949–51 and at Harvard University from 1951 until his death.

In 1942 Key published *Politics, Parties, and Pressure Groups*, in which he analyzed the part played by organized interests in the political process. His *Southern Politics in State and Nation* (1949) pioneered in the use of quantitative techniques and was a classic in regional political studies. In *Public Opinion and American Democracy* (1961) he analyzed the link between the changing patterns of public opinion and the governmental system. He was vigorous in opposing the idea that voters' preferences are socially determined, and in his posthumous work, *The Responsible Electorate: Rationality in Presidential Voting 1936–60* (1966), he analyzed public opinion data and electoral returns to show what he believed to be the rationality of voters' choices. Other works by Key include *The Techniques of Political Graft in the United States* (1936), *A Primer of Statistics for Political Scientists* (1954), and *American State Politics: An Introduction* (1956). He served as president of the American Political Science Association in 1958–59.

been skilled organizers of opinion who understood the mystery well enough to create majorities on election day." Although the reality of public opinion is now almost universally accepted, there is much variation in the way it is defined, reflecting in large measure the different perspectives from which scholars have approached the subject. Contrasting understandings of public opinion have taken shape over the centuries, especially as new methods of measuring public opinion have been applied to politics, commerce, religion, and social activism.

Political scientists and some historians have tended to emphasize the role of public opinion in government and politics, paying particular attention to its influence on the development of government policy. Indeed, some political scientists have regarded public opinion as equivalent to the national will. In such a limited sense, however, there can be only one public opinion on an issue at any given time.

Sociologists, in contrast, usually conceive of public opinion as a product of social interaction and communication. According to this view, there can be no public opinion on an issue unless members of the public communicate with each other. Even if their individual opinions are quite similar to begin with, their beliefs will not constitute a public opinion until they are conveyed to others in some form, whether through print media, radio, television, the Internet, or telephone or face-to-face conversation. Sociologists also point to the possibility of there being many different public opinions on a given issue at the same time. Although one body of opinion may dominate or reflect government policy, for example, this does not preclude the existence of other organized bodies of opinion on political topics. The sociological approach also recognizes the importance of public opinion in areas that have little or nothing to do with government. The very nature of public opinion, according to the American researcher

WALTER LIPPMANN

(b. Sept. 23, 1889, New York City—d. Dec. 14, 1974,
New York City)

Walter Lippmann was an American newspaper commentator and author who in a 60-year career made himself one of the most widely respected political columnists in the world. While studying at Harvard (B.A., 1909), Lippmann was influenced by the philosophers William James and George Santayana. He helped to found (1914) the liberal weekly magazine *The New Republic* and served as its assistant editor under Herbert David Croly. Through his writings in *The New Republic* and through direct consultation, he influenced Pres. Woodrow Wilson, who is said to have drawn on Lippmann's ideas for the post–World War I settlement plan (Fourteen Points) and for the concept of the League of Nations. Lippmann was briefly (1917) an assistant to Secretary of War Newton D. Baker. Wilson sent him to take part in the negotiations for the Treaty of Versailles (1919).

After writing editorials (1921–29) for the reformist *World*, Lippmann served as its editor (1929–31) and then moved to the *New York Herald Tribune*. On Sept. 8, 1931, his column, "Today and Tomorrow," first appeared. Eventually, it was syndicated in more than 250 newspapers in the United States and about 25 other nations and won two Pulitzer Prizes (1958, 1962). In preparing his commentaries, he traveled throughout the world. His first book, *A Preface to Politics* (1913), was mildly socialistic, but *Drift and Mastery* (1914) was anti-Marxist, and in *The Good Society* (1937) he repudiated socialism entirely. During World War II he warned against a postwar return of the United States to an isolationist policy. *Essays in the Public Philosophy* (1955) evoked some criticism for its natural-law theory.

In perhaps his most influential book, *Public Opinion* (1922; reissued 1956), Lippmann seemed to imply that ordinary citizens can no longer judge public issues rationally, since the speed and condensation required in the mass media tend to produce slogans rather than interpretations. In *The Phantom Public* (1925) he again treated the problem of communication in politics. While continuing to doubt the possibility of a true democracy, he nonetheless rejected government by an elite.

Walter Lippmann. Harris & Ewing Collection/Library of Congress, Washington, D.C. (Digital File Number: LC-DIG-hec-21696)

Irving Crespi, is to be interactive, multidimensional, and continuously changing. Thus, fads and fashions are appropriate subject matter for students of public opinion, as are public attitudes toward celebrities or corporations.

Nearly all scholars of public opinion, regardless of the way they may define it, agree that, in order for a phenomenon to count as public opinion, at least four conditions must be satisfied: (1) there must be an issue, (2) there must be a significant number of individuals who express opinions on the issue, (3) there must be some kind of a consensus among at least some of these opinions, and (4) this consensus must directly or indirectly exert influence.

In contrast to scholars, those who aim to influence public opinion are less concerned with theoretical issues than with the practical problem of shaping the opinions of specified "publics," such as employees, stockholders, neighbourhood associations, or any other group whose actions may affect the fortunes of a client or stakeholder. Politicians and publicists, for example, seek ways to influence voting and purchasing decisions, respectively—hence their wish to determine any attitudes and opinions that may affect the desired behaviour.

It is often the case that opinions expressed in public differ from those expressed in private. Some views—even though widely shared—may not be expressed at all. Thus, in a totalitarian state, a great many people may be opposed to the government but may fear to express their attitudes even to their families and friends. In such cases, an anti-government public opinion necessarily fails to develop.

THE FORMATION AND CHANGE OF PUBLIC OPINION

No matter how collective views (those held by most members of a defined public) coalesce into public opinion, the result can be self-perpetuating. The French political scientist Alexis de Tocqueville, for example, observed that once an opinion:

> *has taken root among a democratic people and established itself in the minds of the bulk of the community, it afterwards persists by itself and is maintained without effort, because no one attacks it.*

In 1993 the German opinion researcher Elizabeth Noelle-Neumann characterized this phenomenon as a "spiral of silence," noting that people who perceive that they hold a minority view will be less inclined to express it in public.

Alexis de Tocqueville, detail of an oil painting by T. Chassériau; in the Versailles Museum. H. Roger-Viollet

COMPONENTS OF PUBLIC OPINION

How many people actually form opinions on a given issue, as well as what sorts of opinions they form, depends partly on their immediate situations, partly on more-general social-environmental factors, and partly on their preexisting knowledge, attitudes, and values. Because attitudes and values play such a crucial role in the development of public opinion, scholars of the subject are naturally interested in the nature of these phenomena, as well as in ways to assess their variability and intensity.

The concepts of opinion, attitude, and value used in public opinion research were given an influential metaphorical characterization by the American-born political analyst Robert Worcester, who founded the London-based polling firm MORI (Market & Opinion Research International Ltd.). Values, he suggested, are "the deep tides of public mood, slow to change, but powerful." Opinions, in contrast, are "the ripples on the surface of the public's consciousness—shallow and easily changed." Finally, attitudes are "the currents below the surface, deeper and stronger," representing a midrange between values and opinions. According to Worcester, the art of understanding public opinion rests not only on the measurement of people's views but also on understanding the motivations behind those views.

No matter how strongly they are held, attitudes are subject to change if the individual holding them learns of new facts or perspectives that challenge his or her earlier thinking. This is especially likely when people learn of a contrary position held by an individual whose judgment they respect. This course of influence, known as "opinion leadership," is frequently utilized by publicists as a means of inducing people to reconsider—and quite possibly change—their own views.

Some opinion researchers have contended that the standard technical concept of attitude is not useful for understanding public opinion, because it is insufficiently complex. Crespi, for example, preferred to speak of "attitudinal systems," which he characterized as the combined development of four sets of phenomena: (1) values and interests, (2) knowledge and beliefs, (3) feelings, and (4) behavioral intentions (i.e., conscious inclinations to act in certain ways).

Perhaps the most important concept in public opinion research is that of values. Values are of considerable importance in determining whether people will form opinions on a particular topic. In general, they are more likely to do so when they perceive that their values require it. Values are adopted early in life, in many cases from parents and schools. They are not likely to change, and they strengthen as people grow older. They encompass beliefs about religion—including belief (or disbelief) in God—political outlook, moral standards, and the like. As Worcester's analogy suggests, values are relatively resistant to ordinary attempts at persuasion and to influence by the media, and they rarely shift as a result of positions or arguments expressed in a single debate. Yet they can be shaped—and in some cases completely changed—by prolonged exposure to conflicting values, by concerted thought and discussion, by the feeling that one is "out of step" with others whom one knows and respects, and by the development of significantly new evidence or circumstances.

THE FORMATION OF ATTITUDES

Once an issue is generally recognized, some people will begin to form attitudes about it. If an attitude is expressed to others by sufficient numbers of people, a public opinion on the topic begins to emerge. Not all people will develop a particular attitude about a public issue: some may not be interested, and others simply may not hear about it.

The attitudes that are formed may be held for various reasons. Thus, among people who oppose higher property taxes, one group may be unable to afford them, another may wish to deny additional tax revenues to welfare recipients, another may disagree with a certain government policy, and another may wish to protest what it sees as wasteful government spending. A seemingly homogeneous body of public opinion may therefore be composed of individual opinions that are rooted in very different interests and values. If an attitude does not serve a function such as one of the above, it is unlikely to be formed; an attitude must be useful in some way to the person who holds it.

FACTORS INFLUENCING PUBLIC OPINION

Public opinion is subject to a variety of influences, including the individual's social environment, the operations of the mass media, the activities of interest groups, the existence of opinion leaders, and complex combinations of other factors, including specific historical events.

ENVIRONMENTAL FACTORS

Environmental factors play a critical part in the development of opinions and attitudes. Most pervasive is the influence of the social environment: family, friends, neighbourhood, workplace, place of worship, or school. People usually adjust their attitudes to conform to those that are most prevalent in the social groups to which they belong. Researchers have found, for example, that if a person in the United States who considers himself a liberal becomes surrounded in his home or at his place of work by people who profess conservatism, he is more likely to start voting for conservative candidates than is a liberal whose family and friends share his political views. Similarly, it was found during World War II that men in the U.S. military who transferred from one unit to another often adjusted their opinions to conform more closely to those of the unit to which they were transferred.

THE MASS MEDIA

Newspapers, radio, television, e-mail, and blogs are usually less influential than the individual's social environment (which, nevertheless, may be constituted in part by interactions conducted through Internet-based social media, such as Twitter). These forms of mass media are still significant, however, especially in affirming attitudes and opinions that are already established. The news media focus the public's attention on certain personalities and issues, leading many people to form opinions about them. Government officials accordingly have noted that communications to them from the public tend to "follow the headlines."

The mass media can also reinforce latent attitudes and "activate" them, prompting people to take action. Just before an election, for example, voters who earlier had only a mild preference for one party or candidate may be inspired by media coverage not only to take the trouble to vote but perhaps also to contribute money or to help a party organization in some other way.

The mass media play another important role by letting individuals know what other people think and by giving political leaders large audiences. In this way the media make it possible for public opinion to encompass large numbers of individuals and wide geographic areas. It appears, in fact, that in some European countries the growth of broadcasting, especially television, affected the operation of the parliamentary system. Before television, national elections were seen largely as contests between a number of candidates or parties for parliamentary seats. As the electronic media grew more sophisticated technologically, elections increasingly assumed the appearance of a personal struggle between the leaders of the principal parties concerned. In the United States, presidential candidates have come to personify their parties. Once in office, a president can easily appeal to a national audience over the heads of elected legislative representatives.

In areas where the mass media are thinly spread, as in developing countries or in countries where the media are strictly controlled, word of mouth can sometimes perform the same functions as the press and broadcasting, though on a more limited scale. In developing countries, it is common for those who are literate to read from newspapers to those who are not, or for large numbers of persons to gather around the village radio or a community television. Word of mouth in the marketplace or neighbourhood then carries the information farther. In countries where important news is suppressed by the government, a great deal of information is transmitted by rumour. Word of mouth (or other forms of person-to-person communication, such as Twitter and text messaging) thus becomes the vehicle for underground public opinion in totalitarian countries.

INTEREST GROUPS

Interest groups, nongovernmental organizations (NGOs), religious groups, and labour unions cultivate the formation and spread of public opinion on issues of concern to their constituencies. These groups may be concerned with political, economic, or ideological issues, and most work through the mass media as well as by word of mouth. Some of the larger or more affluent interest groups around the world make use of advertising and public relations. One increasingly popular tactic is the informal poll or straw vote. In this approach, groups ask their members and supporters to "vote"—usually by phone or via the Internet—in unsystematic "polls" of public opinion that are not carried out with proper sampling procedures. Multiple votes by supporters are often encouraged, and once the group releases its findings to credible media outlets, it claims legitimacy by citing the publication of its poll in a recognized newspaper or online news source.

Reasons for conducting unscientific polls range from their entertainment value to their usefulness in manipulating public opinion, especially by interest groups or issue-specific organizations, some of which exploit straw-poll results as a means of making their causes appear more significant than they actually are. On any given issue, however, politicians will weigh the relatively disinterested opinions and attitudes of the majority against the committed values of smaller but more-dedicated groups for whom retribution at the ballot box is more likely.

Woodrow Wilson. Encyclopædia Britannica, Inc.

OPINION LEADERS

Opinion leaders play a major role in defining popular issues and in influencing individual opinions regarding them. Political leaders in particular can turn a relatively unknown problem into a national issue if they decide to call attention to it in the media. One of the ways in which opinion leaders rally opinion and smooth out differences among those who are in basic agreement

PUBLIC OPINION POLLING

Public opinion polling can provide a fairly exact analysis of the distribution of opinions on almost any issue within a given population. Assuming that the proper questions are asked, polling can reveal something about the intensity with which opinions are held, the reasons for these opinions, and the probability that the issues have been discussed with others. Polling can occasionally reveal whether the people holding an opinion can be thought of as constituting a cohesive group. However, survey findings do not provide much information about the opinion leaders who may have played an important part in developing the opinion.

Polls are good tools for measuring "what" or "how much." Finding out "how" or "why," however, is the principal function of qualitative research—including especially the use of focus groups—which involves observing interactions between a limited number of people rather than posing a series of questions to an individual in an in-depth interview. However, polls cannot identify the likely future actions of the public in general, nor can they predict the future behaviour of individuals. One of the best predictors of how people will vote is, simply, the vote that they cast in the last election.

Polls may serve a variety of purposes. Those reported in the media, for example, may be used to inform, to entertain, or to educate. In an election, well-run polls may constitute one of the most systematic and objective sources of political information. They are also the means by which journalists, politicians, business leaders, and other elites—whether they admit it or not—learn what the general public is thinking (other sources include casual encounters with ordinary citizens, listening to callers on radio talk shows, and reading communications from concerned citizens).

Ideally, the people who prepare surveys and carry them out have no mission other than the objective and systematic measurement of public opinion. It is nonetheless possible for bias to enter into the polling process at any point, especially in cases where the entity commissioning the poll has a financial or political interest in the result or wishes to use the result to promote a specific agenda. Polls have been skewed from the outset by news companies surveying public opinion on political issues, by manufacturing firms engaged in market research, by interest groups seeking to popularize their views, and even by academic scholars wishing to inform or influence public discourse about some significant social or scientific issue.

on a subject is by inventing symbols or coining slogans. For instance, in the words of U.S. Pres. Woodrow Wilson, the Allies in World War I were fighting "a war to end all wars," while aiming "to make the world safe for democracy." Post–World War II relations between the U.S. and the Soviet Union were summed up in the term "Cold War," first used by U.S. presidential adviser Bernard Baruch in 1947. Once enunciated, symbols and slogans are frequently kept alive and communicated to large audiences by the mass media and may become the cornerstone of public opinion on any given issue.

Opinion leadership is not confined to prominent figures in public life. An opinion leader can be any person to whom others look for guidance on a certain subject. Thus, within a given social group one person may be regarded as especially well-informed about local politics, another as knowledgeable about foreign affairs, and another as expert in real estate. These local opinion leaders are generally unknown outside their own circle of friends and acquaintances, but their cumulative influence in the formation of public opinion is substantial.

BERNARD BARUCH

(b. Aug. 19, 1870, Camden, S.C., U.S.—d. June 20, 1965, New York, N.Y.)

Bernard Baruch was an American financier who served as an adviser to U.S. presidents.

After graduating from the College of the City of New York in 1889, Baruch worked as an office boy in a linen business and later in Wall Street brokerage houses. Over the years he amassed a fortune as a stock market speculator.

In 1916 he was appointed by Pres. Woodrow Wilson to the Advisory Commission of the Council of National Defense, and during World War I he became chairman of the War Industries Board. In 1919 he was a member of the Supreme Economic Council at the Versailles Peace Conference and was

Bernard Baruch, 1919. Library of Congress, Washington, D.C.

also a personal adviser to Pres. Wilson on the terms of peace. As an expert in wartime economic mobilization, Baruch was employed as an adviser by Pres. Franklin D. Roosevelt during World War II, although he did not hold an administrative position. After the war Baruch played an instrumental role in formulating policy at the United Nations regarding the international control of atomic energy. The designation of "elder statesman" was applied to him perhaps more often than to any other American of his time.

COMPLEX INFLUENCES

Because psychological makeup, personal circumstances, and external influences all play a role in the formation of each person's opinions, it is difficult to predict how public opinion on an issue will take shape. The same is true with regard to changes in public opinion. Some public opinions can be explained by specific events and circumstances, but in other cases the causes are more elusive. (Some opinions, however, are predictable: the public's opinions about other countries, for example, seem to depend largely on the state of relations between the governments involved. Hostile public attitudes do not cause poor relations—they are the result of them.)

People presumably change their own attitudes when they no longer seem to correspond with prevailing circumstances and, hence, fail to serve as guides to action. Similarly, a specific event, such as a natural disaster or a human tragedy, can heighten awareness of underlying problems or concerns and trigger changes in public opinion. Public opinion about the environment, for instance, has been influenced by single events such as the publication of Rachel Carson's *Silent Spring* in 1962; by the toxic gas leak in Bhopal, India, in 1984; by the nuclear accident at Chernobyl, Ukraine, in 1986; by the spill from the oil tanker *Exxon Valdez* in 1989; by the Deepwater Horizon oil spill in the Gulf of Mexico in 2010; and by the Fukushima nuclear accident in Japan in 2011. It is nonetheless the case that whether a body of public opinion on a given issue is formed and sustained depends to a significant extent on the attention it receives in the mass media.

Some changes in public opinion have been difficult for experts to explain. During the second half of the 20th century in many parts of the world, attitudes toward religion, family, sex, international relations, social welfare, and the economy underwent major shifts. Although important issues have claimed public attention in all these areas, the scope of change in public attitudes and opinions is difficult to attribute to any major event or even to any complex of events.

PUBLIC OPINION AND GOVERNMENT

By its very nature, the democratic process spurs citizens to form opinions on a number of issues. Voters are called upon to choose candidates in elections, to consider constitutional amendments, and to approve or reject municipal taxes and other legislative proposals. Almost any matter on which the executive or legislature has to decide may become a public issue if a significant number of people wish to make it one. The political attitudes of these persons are often stimulated or reinforced by outside agencies—a crusading newspaper, an interest group, or a government agency or official.

The English philosopher and economist Jeremy Bentham (1748–1832) saw the greatest difficulty of the legislator as being "in conciliating the public opinion, in correcting it when erroneous, and in giving it that bent which shall be most favourable to produce

Jeremy Bentham, detail of an oil painting by H.W. Pickersgill, 1829; in the National Portrait Gallery, London. Courtesy of the National Portrait Gallery, London

obedience to his mandates." At the same time, Bentham and some other thinkers believed that public opinion is a useful check on the authority of rulers. Bentham demanded that all official acts be publicized, so that an enlightened public opinion could pass judgment on them, as would a tribunal: "To the pernicious exercise of the power of government it is the only check."

In the early years of modern democracy, some scholars acknowledged the power of public opinion but warned that it could be a dangerous force. Tocqueville was concerned that a government of the masses would become a "tyranny of the majority." But, whether public opinion is regarded as a constructive or a baneful force in a democracy, there are few politicians who are prepared to suggest in public that government should ignore it.

Political scientists have been less concerned with what part public opinion should play in a democratic polity and have given more attention to establishing what part it does play in actuality. From the examination of numerous histories of policy formation, it is clear that no sweeping generalization can be made that will hold in all cases. The role of public opinion varies from issue to issue, just as public opinion asserts itself differently from one democracy to another. Perhaps the safest generalization that can be made is that, although public opinion does not influence the details of most government policies, it does set limits within which policy makers must operate. That is, public officials will usually seek to satisfy a widespread demand—or at least take it into account in their deliberations—and they will usually try to avoid decisions that they believe will be widely unpopular.

Yet efforts by political leaders to accommodate government policies to public opinion are not always perceived as legitimate. Indeed, journalists and political commentators have often characterized them as "pandering" to public opinion to curry favour with their constituents or as being driven by the latest poll results. Such charges were questioned, however, by public opinion scholars Lawrence R. Jacobs and Robert Y. Shapiro, who argued that politicians do not actually do this. They found instead that by the early 1970s the accusation of pandering was being used deliberately by prominent journalists, politicians, and other elites as a means of reducing the influence of public opinion on government policy. This practice, they theorized, might have resulted from long-standing suspicion or hostility among elites toward popular participation in government and politics. In keeping with their findings, Jacobs and Shapiro postulated the eventual disappearance from public discourse of the stigmatizing term *pandering* and its replacement by the more neutral term *political responsiveness*.

Although they rejected the charge of pandering, Jacobs and Shapiro also asserted that most politicians tend to respond to public opinion in cynical ways. Most of them, for example, use public opinion research not to establish their policies but only to identify slogans and symbols that will make predetermined policies more appealing to their constituents. According to Jacobs and Shapiro, most public opinion research is used to manipulate the public rather than to act on its wishes.

Public opinion exerts a more powerful influence in politics through its "latent" aspects. As discussed by V.O. Key, Jr., latent public opinion is, in effect, a probable future reaction by the public to a current decision or action by a public official or a government. Politicians who ignore the possible consequences of latent public opinion risk setback or defeat in future elections. Government leaders who take latent public opinion into account, on the other hand, may be willing to undertake an unpopular action that has a negative effect on public opinion in the near term, provided that the action is also likely to have a sig-nificant positive effect at a later and more important time.

Public opinion seems to be much more effective in influencing policy making at the local level than at the state or national levels. One reason for this is that issues of concern to local governments — such as the condition of roads, schools, and hospitals — are less complex than those dealt with by governments at higher levels. Another is that at the local level there are fewer institutional or bureaucratic barriers between policy makers and voters. Representative government itself, however, tends to limit the power of public opinion to influence specific govern-ment decisions, since ordinarily the only choice the public is given is that of approving or disapproving the election of a particular official.

A n election is a formal process of selecting a person for public office or of accepting or rejecting a political proposition by voting. It is important to distinguish between the form and the substance of elections. In some cases, electoral forms are present but the substance of an election is missing, as when voters do not have a free and

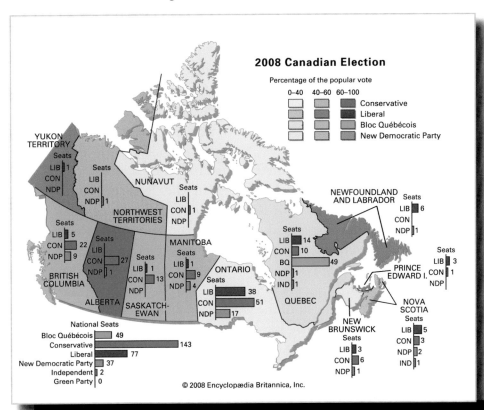

Canada's 2008 federal election results. Encyclopædia Britannica, Inc.

genuine choice between at least two alternatives. Most countries hold elections in at least the formal sense, but in many of them the elections are not competitive (e.g., all but one party may be forbidden to contest) or the electoral situation is in other respects highly compromised.

THE HISTORY OF ELECTIONS

Although elections were used in ancient Athens, in Rome, and in the selection of popes and Holy Roman emperors, the origins of elections in the contemporary world lie in the gradual emergence of representative government in Europe and North America beginning in the 17th century. At that time, the holistic notion of representation characteristic of the Middle Ages was transformed into a more individualistic conception, one that made the individual the critical unit to be counted. For example, the British Parliament was no longer seen as representing estates, corporations, and vested interests but, rather, was perceived as standing for actual human beings. The movement abolishing the so-called "rotten boroughs"—electoral districts of small population controlled by a single person or family—that culminated in the Reform Act of 1832 (one of three major Reform Bills in the 19th century in Britain that expanded the size of the electorate) was a direct consequence of this individualistic conception of representation.

Once governments were believed to derive their powers from the consent of the governed and expected to seek that consent regularly, it remained to decide precisely who was to be included among the governed whose consent was necessary. Advocates of full democracy favoured the establishment of universal adult suffrage. Across western Europe and North America, adult male suffrage was

ensured almost everywhere by 1920, though woman suffrage was not established until somewhat later (e.g., 1928
in Britain, 1944 in France, 1949 in Belgium, and 1971 in
Switzerland).

Although it is common to equate representative government and elections with democracy, and although
competitive elections under universal suffrage are one
of democracy's defining characteristics, universal suffrage is not a necessary condition of competitive electoral
politics. An electorate may be limited by formal legal
requirements—as was the case before universal adult suffrage—or it may be limited by the failure of citizens to
exercise their right to vote. In many countries with free
elections, large numbers of citizens do not cast ballots. For
example, in Switzerland and the United States, fewer than
half the electorate vote in most elections. Although legal
or self-imposed exclusion can dramatically affect public
policy and even undermine the legitimacy of a government, it does not preclude decision making by election,
provided that voters are given genuine alternatives among
which to choose.

During the 18th century, access to the political arena
depended largely on membership in an aristocracy, and
participation in elections was regulated mainly by local
customs and arrangements. Although both the American
and French revolutions declared every citizen formally
equal to every other, the vote remained an instrument of
political power possessed by very few.

Even with the implementation of universal suffrage,
the ideal of "one person, one vote" was not achieved in
all countries. Systems of plural voting were maintained in
some countries, giving certain social groups an electoral
advantage. For example, in the United Kingdom, university graduates and owners of businesses in constituencies

other than those in which they lived could cast more than one ballot until 1948. Before World War I, both Austria and Prussia had three classes of weighted votes that effectively kept electoral power in the hands of the upper social strata. Until the passage of the Voting Rights Act in 1965 in the United States, legal barriers and intimidation effectively barred most African Americans—especially those in the South—from being able to cast ballots in elections.

During the 19th and 20th centuries, the increased use of competitive mass elections in western Europe had the purpose and effect of institutionalizing the diversity that had existed in the countries of that region. However, mass elections had quite different purposes and consequences under the one-party communist regimes of eastern Europe and the Soviet Union during the period from the end of World War II to 1989–90. Although these governments held elections, the contests were not competitive, as voters usually had only the choice of voting for or against the official candidate. Indeed, elections in these countries were similar to the 19th-century Napoleonic plebiscites, which were intended to demonstrate the unity rather than the diversity of the people. Dissent in eastern Europe could be registered by crossing out the name of the candidate on the ballot, as several million citizens in the Soviet Union did in each election before 1989. However, because secret voting did not exist in these countries, this practice invited reprisals. Nonvoting was another form of protest, especially as local communist activists were under extreme pressure to achieve nearly a 100 percent turnout. Not all elections in eastern Europe followed the Soviet model. For example, in Poland more names appeared on the ballot than there were offices to fill, and some degree of electoral choice was thus provided.

In sub-Saharan Africa, competitive elections based on universal suffrage were introduced in three distinct

VOTING RIGHTS ACT

The Voting Rights Act (Aug. 6, 1965) was adopted in the United States in order to remove legal barriers at the state and local levels that prevented African Americans from exercising their right to vote.

Shortly following the American Civil War (1861–65), the Fifteenth Amendment (1870) was ratified, guaranteeing that the right to vote would not be denied "on account of race, color, or previous condition of servitude." Soon afterward the U.S. Congress enacted legislation that made it a federal crime to interfere with an individual's right to vote. In some states of the former Confederacy, African Americans became a majority or near majority of the eligible voting population, and African American candidates ran and were elected to office at all levels of government.

Nevertheless, there was strong opposition to the extension of the franchise to African Americans. Following the end of Reconstruction in 1877, the Supreme Court of the United States limited voting protections under federal legislation, and intimidation and fraud were employed by white leaders to reduce voter registration and turnout among African Americans. As whites came to dominate state legislatures once again, poll taxes, literacy tests, grandfather clauses, whites-only primaries, and other measures were introduced to disqualify African Americans from voting. The result was that by the early 20th century nearly all African Americans were disfranchised. Although

Pres. George W. Bush signing the Voting Rights Act Reauthorization, July 2006. Paul Morse/White House photo

the U.S. Supreme Court later declared several such measures unconstitutional, by the early 1960s voter registration rates among African Americans were negligible in much of the Deep South.

In 1964 the Civil Rights Act was passed and the Twenty-fourth Amendment, abolishing poll taxes for voting for federal offices, was ratified. In the following year Congress passed the Voting Rights Act, which suspended literacy tests and provided for federal oversight of voter registration in areas that had previously used tests to determine voter eligibility. An expansion of the law in the 1970s also protected voting rights for non-English-speaking U.S. citizens. The oversight provision of the law was extended for 5 years in 1970, 7 years in 1975, and 25 years in both 1982 and 2006. In what was widely perceived to be a test case, *Northwest Austin Municipal Utility District Number One v. Holder, et al.* (2009), the Supreme Court declined to rule on the constitutionality of the federal-oversight provision of the Voting Rights Act.

periods. In the 1950s and '60s, a number of countries held elections following decolonization. Although many of them reverted to authoritarian forms of rule, there were exceptions (e.g., Botswana and Gambia). In the late 1970s, elections were introduced in a smaller number of countries when some military dictatorships were dissolved (e.g., in Ghana and Nigeria) and other countries in Southern Africa underwent decolonization (e.g., Angola, Mozambique, and Zimbabwe). Beginning in the early 1990s, the end of the Cold War and the reduction of military and economic aid from developed countries brought about democratization and competitive elections in more than a dozen African countries, including Benin, Mali, South Africa, and Zambia.

Competitive elections in Latin America also were introduced in phases. In the century after 1828, for example, elections were held in Argentina, Chile, Colombia, and Uruguay, though all but Chile reverted to authoritarianism. Additional countries held elections in the period dating roughly 1943 to 1962, though again many did not retain democratic governments. Beginning in the mid 1970s, competitive elections were introduced gradually throughout most of Latin America.

In Asia, competitive elections were held following the end of World War II, in many cases as a result of decolonization (e.g., India, Indonesia, Malaysia, and the Philippines), though once again the restoration of authoritarianism was commonplace. Beginning in the 1970s, competitive elections were reintroduced in a number of countries, including the Philippines and South Korea. With the exception of Turkey and Israel, competitive elections in the Middle East were rare.

Authoritarian regimes often have used elections as a way to achieve a degree of popular legitimacy. Dictatorships may hold elections in cases where no substantive opposition is remotely feasible (e.g., because opposition forces have been repressed) or when economic factors favour the regime. Even when opposition parties are allowed to participate, they may face intimidation by the government and its allies, which thereby precludes the effective mobilization of potential supporters. In other cases, a regime may postpone an election if there is a significant chance that it will lose. In addition, it has been a common practice of authoritarian regimes to intervene once balloting has begun by intimidating voters (e.g., through physical attacks) and by manipulating the count of votes that have been freely cast.

FUNCTIONS OF ELECTIONS

Elections make a fundamental contribution to democratic governance. Because direct democracy—a form of government in which political decisions are made directly by the entire body of qualified citizens—is impractical in most modern societies, democratic government must be conducted through representatives. Elections enable voters to select leaders and to hold them accountable for their performance in office. Accountability can be undermined when elected leaders do not care whether they are reelected or when, for historical or other reasons, one party or coalition is so dominant that there is effectively no choice for voters among alternative candidates, parties, or policies. Nevertheless, the possibility of controlling leaders by requiring them to submit to regular and periodic elections helps to solve the problem of succession in leadership and thus contributes to the continuation of democracy. Moreover, where the electoral process is competitive and forces candidates or parties to expose their records and future intentions to popular scrutiny, elections serve as forums for the discussion of public issues and facilitate the expression of public opinion. Elections thus provide political education for citizens and ensure the responsiveness of democratic governments to the will of the people. They also serve to legitimize the acts of those who wield power, a function that is performed to some extent even by elections that are noncompetitive.

Elections also reinforce the stability and legitimacy of the political community. Like national holidays commemorating common experiences, elections link citizens to each other and thereby confirm the viability of the polity. As a result, elections help to facilitate social and political integration.

Finally, elections serve a self-actualizing purpose by confirming the worth and dignity of individual citizens as human beings. Whatever other needs voters may have, participation in an election serves to reinforce their self-esteem and self-respect. Voting gives people an opportunity to have their say and, through expressing partisanship, to satisfy their need to feel a sense of belonging. Even nonvoting satisfies the need of some people to express their alienation from the political community. For precisely these reasons, the long battle for the right to vote and the demand for equality in electoral participation can be viewed as the manifestation of a profound human craving for personal fulfillment.

Whether held under authoritarian or democratic regimes, elections have a ritualistic aspect. Elections

Republican U.S. presidential hopefuls (left to right) *Mitt Romney, Rick Perry, and Ron Paul debating in September 2011. Such forums allow for insight into a candidate's thoughts on public issues.* Kevork Djansezian/Getty Images

and the campaigns preceding them are dramatic events that are accompanied by rallies, banners, posters, buttons, headlines, and television coverage, all of which call attention to the importance of participation in the event. Candidates, political parties, and interest groups representing diverse objectives invoke the symbols of nationalism or patriotism, reform or revolution, past glory or future promise. Whatever the peculiar national, regional, or local variations, elections are events that, by arousing emotions and channeling them toward collective symbols, break the monotony of daily life and focus attention on the common fate.

TYPES OF ELECTIONS

There are four main types of elections. The election of officeholders allows the electorate to vote for individuals to act as their representatives in the governmental process. Recall elections attempt to minimize the influence of political parties on representatives. Elections pertaining to referenda and initiatives let citizens vote on community issues. Finally, plebiscite elections are a vote by the people of an entire country or district to decide on issues such as choice of a ruler or type of government, as well as questions of national policy.

ELECTIONS OF OFFICEHOLDERS

Electorates have only a limited power to determine government policies. Most elections do not directly establish public policy but instead confer on a small group of officials the authority to make policy (through laws and other devices) on behalf of the electorate as a whole.

Political parties are central to the election of officeholders. The selection and nomination of candidates, a vital first stage of the electoral process, generally lies in the hands of political parties; an election serves only as the final process in the recruitment to political office. The party system thus can be regarded as an extension of the electoral process. Political parties provide the pool of talent from which candidates are drawn, and they simplify and direct the electoral choice and mobilize the electorate at the registration and election stage.

The predominance of political parties over the electoral process has not gone unchallenged. For example, some municipalities in the United States and Canada regularly hold nonpartisan elections (in which party affiliations are not formally indicated on ballots) in order to limit the influence of political parties. Nonpartisanship in the United States started as a reform movement in the early 20th century and was intended in part to isolate local politics from politics at the state and national levels. During the last decades of the 20th century, the significance of political parties declined in many democratic countries as "candidate-centred" politics emerged and campaigning and accountability became highly personalized.

RECALL ELECTIONS

Widely adopted in the United States, the recall is designed to ensure that an elected official will act in the interests of his constituency rather than in the interests of his political party or according to his own conscience. The actual instrument of recall is usually a letter of resignation signed by the elected representative before assuming office. During the term of office, the letter can be evoked by a quorum of constituents if the representative's performance fails to meet their expectations.

In the United States the recall has been used successfully against various types of officials, including judges, mayors, and even state governors. Although in practice the recall is not used extensively, even in jurisdictions where it is provided for constitutionally, it has been used to remove governors in North Dakota (1921) and California (2003). Following a bitter partisan fight between Democrats and Republicans over the rights of workers to bargain collectively, Wisconsin experienced in 2011 the single largest recall attempt in U.S. history. Six Republicans and three Democrats in the 33-member state Senate faced a recall vote, though only two senators—both Republicans—were defeated.

REFERENDA AND INITIATIVES

Referenda and initiatives are elections in which the preferences of the community are assessed on a particular issue. Whereas the former are instigated by those in government, the latter are initiated by groups of electors. As forms of direct democracy, such devices reflect a reluctance to entrust full decision-making power to elected representatives. However, because voter turnout in these types of elections often is quite low, voting in referenda and initiatives may be more easily influenced by political parties and interest groups than voting in officeholder elections.

Referenda often are used for bond issues to raise and spend public money, though occasionally they are used to decide certain social or moral issues—such as restrictions on abortion or divorce—on which the elected bodies are deemed to possess no special competence. Referenda may be legislatively binding or merely consultative, but even consultative referenda are likely to be considered legislative mandates.

Referenda and initiatives at the national level have been used most heavily in Switzerland, which has held

Citizens rally to demand the recall of Wisconsin governor Scott Walker in March 2011. A partisan fight over union collective bargaining rights in the state led to the recall push. Justin Sullivan/ Getty Images

about half the world's national referenda. Evidence from Switzerland has shown that referenda brought to a vote by legislators are more likely to succeed than those initiated by the public. For example, about half of all laws and nearly three-fourths of all constitutional amendments initiated by the Swiss government have been passed, whereas only about one-tenth of all citizen initiatives have been successful. Switzerland uses referenda and initiatives extensively at the local and regional levels as well, as does the United States. Near the end of the 20th century, referenda were employed more frequently around the world than in earlier years. This was particularly true in Europe, where referenda were held to decide public policy on voting systems, treaties and peace agreements (e.g., the Treaty on European Union), and social issues.

PLEBISCITES

Plebiscites are elections held to decide two paramount types of political issues: government legitimacy and the nationality of territories contested between governments. In the former case, the incumbent government, seeking a popular mandate as a basis for legitimacy, employs a plebiscite to establish its right to speak for the nation. Plebiscites of this nature are thought to establish a direct link between the rulers and the ruled. Intermediaries such as political parties are bypassed, and for this reason plebiscites are sometimes considered antithetical to pluralism and competitive politics. Following the French Revolution in 1789, the plebiscite was widely popular in France, rooted as it was in the ideas of nationalism and popular sovereignty. In the 20th century, totalitarian regimes employed plebiscites to legitimize their rule.

Plebiscites also have been used as a device for deciding the nationality of territories. For example, after World

Portrait of Napoleon III, French emperor from 1852 to 1870. Elected president of France in 1850, Napoleon III named himself emperor after a plebiscite that revised the country's constitution. Kean Collection/Archive Photos/Getty Images

War I the League of Nations proposed 11 such plebiscites, the most successful of which was held in 1935 in the Saar, until the end of the war a state of Germany that had been administered by the League for 15 years. Its inhabitants chose overwhelmingly to return to Germany rather than to become a part of France. This use of plebiscites, however, is relatively rare, because it requires the prior agreement of the governments involved on an issue that is usually very contentious.

SYSTEMS OF VOTE COUNTING

Individual votes are translated into collective decisions by a wide variety of rules of counting that voters and leaders have accepted as legitimate prior to the election. These rules may in principle call for any of various different forms of voting: (1) plurality voting, which requires only that the winner have the greatest number of votes, (2) absolute majority voting, which requires that the winner receive more than half the total number of votes, (3) extraordinary majority voting, which requires some higher proportion for the winner—e.g., a two-thirds majority—(4) proportional voting, which requires that a political party receive some threshold to receive representation, or (5) unanimity.

LEGISLATIVE ELECTIONS

A wide variety of electoral systems exist for apportioning legislative seats. In practice, legislative electoral systems can be classified into three broad categories: plurality and majority systems (collectively known as majoritarian systems), proportional systems, and hybrid, or semiproportional, systems. The electoral system is an important variable in explaining public policy decisions, because it determines the number of political parties able to receive representation and thereby participate in government.

PLURALITY AND MAJORITY SYSTEMS

The plurality system is the simplest means of determining the outcome of an election. To win, a candidate need only poll more votes than any other single opponent. He need not, as required by the majority formula, poll more votes than the combined opposition. The more candidates contesting a constituency seat, the greater the probability that the winning candidate will receive only a minority of the votes cast. Countries using the plurality formula for national legislative elections include Canada, Great Britain, India, and the United States. Countries with plurality systems usually have had two main parties.

Under the majority system, the party or candidate winning more than 50 percent of the vote in a constituency is awarded the contested seat. A difficulty in systems with the absolute-majority criterion is that it may not be satisfied in contests in which there are more than two candidates. Several variants of the majority formula have been developed to address this problem. In Australia the alternative, or preferential, vote is used in lower-house elections. Voters rank the candidates on an alternative-preference ballot. If a majority is not achieved by first-preference votes, the weakest candidate is eliminated, and that candidate's votes are redistributed to the other candidates according to the second preference on the ballot. This redistributive process is repeated until one candidate has collected a majority of the votes.

In France a double-ballot system is employed for National Assembly elections. If no candidate secures a majority in the first round of elections, another round is required. In the second round, only those candidates securing the votes of at least one-eighth of the registered electorate in the first round may compete, and the candidate securing a plurality of the popular vote in the second round is declared the winner. Some candidates eligible for the second round withdraw their candidacy and endorse one of the leading candidates. In contrast to the two-party norm of the plurality system, France has what some analysts have called a "two-bloc" system, in which the main parties of the left and the main parties of the right compete against each other in the first round of an election to be the representative of their respective ideological group and then ally with one another to maximize their bloc's representation in the second round. An infrequently used variant is the supplementary-vote system, which was instituted for London mayoral elections. Under this system,

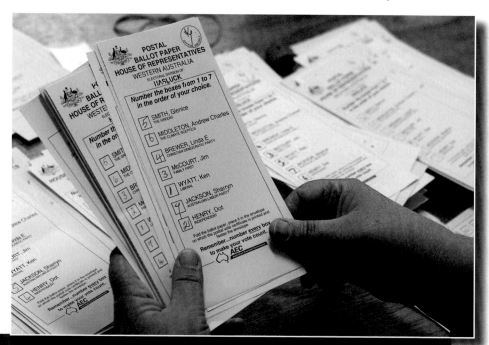

Absentee paper ballots, ranking candidates using the preferential vote system, are reviewed during Australia's 2010 federal elections. Paul Kane/Getty Images

voters rank their top two preferences, and, in the event that no candidate wins a majority of first-preference votes, all ballots not indicating the top two vote getters as either a first or a second choice are discarded, and the combination of first and second preferences is used to determine the winner. Majority formulas usually are applied only within single-member electoral constituencies.

The majority and the plurality formulas do not always distribute legislative seats in proportion to the share of the popular vote won by the competing parties. Both formulas tend to reward the strongest party disproportionately and to handicap weaker parties, though these parties may escape the inequities of the system if their support is regionally concentrated. For example, in national elections in Britain in 2001, the Labour Party captured more than three-fifths of the seats in the House of Commons, even though it won barely two-fifths of the popular vote. In contrast, the Conservative Party won one-fourth of the seats with nearly one-third of the vote. Third-party representation varied considerably: whereas the Liberal Democrats, whose support was spread throughout the country, captured 8 percent of the seats with more than 18 percent of the vote, the Plaid Cymru, whose support is concentrated wholly in Wales, won 0.7 percent of the vote and 0.7 percent of the seats. The plurality formula usually, though not always, distorts the distribution of seats more than the majority system.

PROPORTIONAL REPRESENTATION

Proportional representation requires that the distribution of seats broadly be proportional to the distribution of the popular vote among competing political parties. It seeks to overcome the disproportionalities that result from majority and plurality formulas and to create a representative body that reflects the distribution of opinion within the electorate. Because of the use of multimember constituencies in proportional representation, parties with neither a majority nor a plurality of the popular vote can still win legislative representation. Consequentially, the number of political parties represented in the legislature often is large. For example, in Israel there are usually more than 10 parties in the Knesset.

Although approximated in many systems, proportionality can never be perfectly realized. Not surprisingly, the outcomes of proportional systems usually are more proportional than those of plurality or majority systems. Nevertheless, a number of factors can generate disproportional outcomes even under proportional representation. The single most important factor determining the actual proportionality of a proportional system is the "district magnitude"—that is, the number of candidates that an individual constituency elects. The larger the number of seats per electoral district, the more proportional the outcome. A second important factor is the specific formula used to translate votes into seats. There are two basic types of formula: single transferable vote and party-list proportional representation.

THE SINGLE TRANSFERABLE VOTE

Developed in the 19th century in Denmark and in Britain, the single transferable vote formula—or Hare system, after one of its English developers, Thomas Hare—employs a ballot that allows the voter to rank candidates in order of preference. When the ballots are counted, any candidate receiving the necessary quota of first preference votes—calculated as one plus the number of votes divided by the number of seats plus one—is awarded a seat. In the electoral calculations, votes received by a winning candidate in excess of the quota are transferred to other candidates according to the second preference marked on the ballot. Any candidate who then achieves the necessary quota is also awarded a seat. This process is repeated, with subsequent surpluses also being transferred, until all the remaining seats have been awarded. Five-member constituencies are considered optimal for the operation of the single transferable vote system.

Because it involves the aggregation of ranked preferences, the single transferable vote formula necessitates complex electoral computations. This complexity, as well as the fact that it limits the influence of political parties, probably accounts for its infrequent use. It has been used in Northern Ireland, Ireland, and Malta and in the selection of the Australian and South African senates. The characteristic of the Hare formula that distinguishes it from other proportional representation formulas is its emphasis on candidates, not parties. The party affiliation of the candidates has no bearing on the computations. The success of minor parties varies considerably: small centrist parties usually benefit from the vote transfers, but small extremist parties usually are penalized.

PARTY-LIST PROPORTIONAL REPRESENTATION

The basic difference between the single transferable vote formula and list systems—which predominate in elections in western Europe and Latin America—is that, in the latter, voters generally choose among party-compiled lists of candidates rather than among individual candidates. Although voters may have some limited choice among individual candidates, electoral computations are made on the basis of party affiliation, and seats are awarded on the basis of party rather than candidate totals. The seats that a party wins are allocated to its candidates in the order in which they appear on the party list. Several types of electoral formulas are used, but there are two main types: largest-average and greatest-remainder formulas.

In the largest-average formula, the available seats are awarded one at a time to the party with the largest average number of votes as determined by dividing the number of votes won by the party by the number of seats the party has been awarded plus a certain integer, depending upon the method used. Each time a party wins a seat, the divisor for that party increases by the same integer, which thus reduces its chances of winning the next seat. Under all methods, the first seat is awarded to the party with the largest absolute number of votes, since, no seats having been allocated, the average vote total as determined by the formula will be largest for this party. Under the d'Hondt method, named after its Belgian inventor, Victor d'Hondt, the average is determined by dividing the number of votes by the number of seats plus one. Thus, after the first seat is awarded, the number of votes won by that party is divided by two (equal to the initial divisor plus one), and similarly for the party awarded the second seat, and so on. Under the so-called Sainte-Laguë method, developed by Andre Sainte-Laguë of France, only odd numbers are used. After a party has won its first seat, its vote total is divided by three; after it wins subsequent seats, the divisor is increased by two. The d'Hondt formula is used in Austria, Belgium, Finland, and the Netherlands, and the Sainte-Laguë method is used in Denmark, Norway, and Sweden.

The d'Hondt formula has a slight tendency to overreward large parties and to reduce the ability of small parties to gain legislative representation. In contrast, the Sainte-Laguë method reduces the reward to large parties, and it generally has benefited middle-size parties at the expense of both large and small parties. Proposals have been made to divide lists by fractions (e.g., 1.4, 2.5, and so on) rather than integers to provide the most proportional result possible.

The greatest-remainder method first establishes a quota that is necessary for a party to receive representation. Formulas vary, but they are generally some variation of dividing the total vote in the district by the number of seats. The total popular vote won by each party is divided by the quota, and a seat is awarded as many times as the party total contains the full quota. If all the seats are awarded in this manner, the election is complete. However, such an outcome is unlikely. Seats that are not won by full quotas subsequently are awarded to the parties with the largest remainder of votes after the quota has been subtracted from each party's total vote for each seat it was awarded. Seats are distributed sequentially to the parties with the largest remainder until all the district's allocated seats have been awarded.

Minor parties generally fare better under the greatest-remainder formula than under the largest-average formula. The greatest-remainder formula is used in Israel and Luxembourg and for some seats in the Danish Folketing. Prior to 1994 Italy used a special variant of the greatest-remainder formula, called the Imperiali formula, whereby the electoral quota was established by dividing the total popular vote by the number of seats plus two. This modification increased the legislative representation of small parties but led to a greater distortion of the proportional ideal.

The proportionality of outcomes also can be diluted by the imposition of an electoral threshold that requires a political party to exceed some minimum percentage of the vote to receive representation. Designed to limit the political success of small extremist parties, such thresholds can constitute significant obstacles to representation. The threshold varies by country, having been set at 4 percent in Sweden, 5 percent in Germany, and 10 percent in Turkey.

HYBRID SYSTEMS

In some countries, the majoritarian and proportional systems are combined into what are called mixed-member proportional or additional-members systems. Although there are a number of variants, all mixed-member proportional systems elect some representatives by proportional representation and the remainder by a nonproportional formula. The classic example of the hybrid system is the German Bundestag, which combines the personal link between representatives and voters with proportionality. The German constitution provides for the election of half the country's parliamentarians by proportional representation and half by simple plurality voting in single-member constituencies. Each voter casts two ballots. The first vote (*Erstimme*) is cast for an individual to represent a constituency (*Wahlkreise*); the candidate receiving the most votes wins the election. The second vote (*Zweitstimme*) is cast for a regional party list. The results of the second vote determine the overall political complexion of the Bundestag. All parties that receive at least 5 percent of the national vote—or win at least three constituencies—are allocated seats on the basis of the percentage of votes that they receive. The votes of parties not receiving representation are reapportioned to the larger parties on the basis of their share of the vote. During the 1990s, a number of countries adopted variants of the German system, including Italy, Japan, New Zealand, and several eastern European countries (e.g., Hungary, Russia, and Ukraine). A hybrid system also was adopted by the British government for devolved assemblies in Scotland and Wales. One of the chief differences between mixed-member systems is the percentage of seats allocated by proportional and majoritarian methods. For example, in Italy and Japan, respectively, roughly three-fourths and three-fifths of all seats are apportioned through constituency elections.

A country's choice of electoral system, like its conception of representation, generally reflects its particular cultural, social, historical, and political circumstances. Majority or plural methods of voting are most likely to be acceptable in relatively stable political cultures. In such cultures, fluctuations in electoral support from one election to the next reduce polarization and encourage political centrism. Thus, the "winner take all" implications of the majority or plurality formulas are not experienced as unduly deprivational or restrictive. In contrast, proportional representation is more likely to be found in societies with traditional ethnic, linguistic, and religious cleavages or in societies that have experienced class and ideological conflicts.

EXECUTIVE ELECTIONS

Although some executives still attain their position by heredity, most are now elected. Elections can be accomplished by a legislature, as in parliamentary systems, or independently, as in presidential and semipresidential systems.

PARLIAMENTARY SYSTEMS

In most parliamentary systems, the head of government is selected by the legislature. To reduce the influence of minor parties over the formation of governments in the Knesset, in 1992 Israel adopted a unique system that called for the direct election of the prime minister by a plurality vote of the public. Owing to the unanticipated further splintering of the political system, however, legislators later voted to restore their role in selecting the prime minister. Parliamentary systems that have, in addition to a prime minister, a less-powerful nonhereditary president have adopted different methods for his election. For example, in Germany the president is selected by both the upper and the lower chamber of the legislature. By contrast, in Ireland the president is elected by a plurality vote of the public.

PRESIDENTIAL AND SEMIPRESIDENTIAL SYSTEMS

In presidential systems and mixed (semipresidential) systems, the head of state is elected independently of the legislature. Several methods of electing presidents have

Members of a young-voters group in New York City colour maps of the United States to reflect results of the electoral college vote during the 2008 presidential election. Bloomberg via Getty Images

been adopted. In the simplest method, the plurality system, which is used in Mexico and the Philippines, the candidate with the most votes wins election. In France the president is required to win a majority. If no candidate receives a majority of the votes cast in the first round of balloting, the top two candidates from the first round proceed to the second round, which is held two weeks later. This system also has been used in presidential elections in Ghana, Peru, and Russia; Nicaragua adopted a variant of this model that allows a candidate to avoid a runoff with a minimum of 45 percent of the vote in the first round.

Both the plurality and the majority-decision rules are employed in the election of U.S. presidents, who are elected only indirectly by the public. The composition of the electoral college, which actually selects the president, is determined by a plurality vote taken within each state. Although voters choose between the various presidential candidates, they are in effect choosing the electors who will elect the president by means of a majority vote in the electoral college. With the exception of Maine and Nebraska, all of a state's electoral votes (which are equal in number to its seats in Congress) are awarded to the presidential candidate who gains a plurality of the vote in the state election. It is thus possible for a president to be elected with a minority of the popular vote, as happened in the presidential elections of 1876 (won by Rutherford B. Hayes), 1888 (won by Benjamin Harrison), and 2000 (won by George W. Bush).

CONSTITUENCIES: DISTRICTING AND APPORTIONMENT

The drawing up of constituencies—the subdivisions of the total electorate that send representatives to the local or central assembly—is inextricably linked with questions about the nature of representation and methods of voting. The problem of electoral representation hinges on the question of what is to be represented. As geographic areas, constituencies often contain within their boundaries diverse, and sometimes incompatible, social, economic, religious, or ethnic interests, all of which seek to be represented.

The solution to this problem has been largely historically determined. Where the interests of electors have not been totally incompatible, and where ethnic, religious, social, and economic differences have been relatively free of passionate conflict, as in the Anglo-American countries, geographic areas (electoral districts) have usually been considered the constituency, and the method of counting has been some system of majority or plurality voting. The elected person represents the whole geographic unit, irrespective of internal divisions. In general, such countries have adopted single-seat constituencies, though multi-member constituencies are also possible.

In contrast, where the electorate is composed of several minorities, none of which can hope to obtain a majority, or perhaps not even a plurality sufficiently large to obtain representation, the geographic district can be regarded only as an administrative unit for counting votes. The effective constituency is the group of electors that can be identified as having voted for a given candidate. In this case, election is usually by some method of proportional counting whereby any candidate, party, or group receiving a requisite number of votes is entitled to a proportionate number of representatives.

The drawing up, or delimitation, of electoral districts is linked with differing conceptions of representation, and conceptions of representation in turn are linked with alternative methods of vote counting. The virtues and vices of different electoral arrangements have long been debated by framers of constitutions and advocates of electoral reform. Although proportional systems treating electoral districts as merely administrative conveniences and providing for multiple representation are believed to approximate more closely the one person, one vote principle of democratic theory than do single-member geographic constituencies providing for majority or plurality voting, they are sometimes criticized for contributing to governmental instability and political stalemate. Critics have cited the "immobilist" regimes of Weimar Germany (1919–33), the French Fourth Republic (1946–58), and post–World War II Italy—all of which had proportional-representation systems and frequent changes of government—as examples. Against this, however, there are numerous instances of politically stable democracies that use proportional representation—e.g., Germany since World War II, the Netherlands, and Switzerland. In any case, it is doubtful that any other method of electoral districting and vote counting would be satisfactory in countries with many interests seeking representation.

Furthermore, representation of geographic constituencies by majority or plurality voting disguises many differences in the electorate's composition and preferences. In single-member, majority-vote electoral districts, the minority that loses at the polls may feel unrepresented. It is even a precarious assumption that the majority itself is truly represented, as it is likely to be a loose coalition of diverse interests, and no single representative can usually do justice to the diversity of interests involved. In general, therefore, the representative, insofar as he is responsive, is more likely to play the role of broker between his district's diverse interests than to fill the role of representative of the district as a whole.

Whatever the role of the representative, and however electoral units are conceived—as geographic areas with stable, compatible interests or as purely administrative areas for the purpose of vote counting—districting must be distinguished from apportionment. In general, if the district is considered only an administrative unit for counting votes, its boundaries can be drawn rather arbitrarily without injustice. The district as such has no stakes of its own to be represented. On the other hand, if the district is considered a true constituency, in the sense that it has unique interests that can be geographically and, as a result, socially defined, districting should not be arbitrary. The area involved should at least be contiguous and compact so that its presumed interests can be fairly recognized.

The difficulty in treating geographic areas as genuine constituencies is that internal transformations in their economic and social structure may make their historical boundaries obsolete. As a result, historical areas serving as electoral districts—such as provinces, states, and counties—may no longer constitute genuine communities of interest to be represented. As these districts become increasingly diverse, it is often difficult to identify particular constituency interests, and representatives find it increasingly impossible to be responsive to constituency wishes or needs.

Problems of apportionment, in contrast to problems of districting, stem from efforts to reconcile the territorial and population bases of representation. If geographic areas, for instance, are assumed to have an equal right to be represented because the area is considered to be a viable constituency, malapportionment in terms of population is inevitable. In the United States, for example, the state of California, with a population of more than 37 million people, has the same number of senators as Wyoming, which has a population of roughly 560,000. This kind of "constitutional malapportionment" must not be confused with the "electoral malapportionment" that defies the one person, one vote principle of equal representation. The latter is usually the result of population shifts.

During the 19th and much of the 20th century, failure to reapportion the number of seats in representative bodies to take account of population changes resulting from increasing urbanization generally benefitted rural electoral districts. More recently, the migration of people from cities to the suburbs has led to possible underrepresentation of suburban populations as against urban ones. From a political rather than a legal perspective, malapportionment is usually considered "undemocratic" because it results in the overrepresentation or underrepresentation of certain sectors of the population and, consequently, may eventuate in public policies not acceptable to the majority of the electorate.

Apportionment is often a complex problem. In particular, it is often unclear how best to define the population among which a specified number of legislative seats are to be apportioned. Any of several distinct quantities—the total population, the number of citizens of voting age, the number of registered voters, or the number of actual voters—may serve as bases of apportionment. If a constant relationship existed between these groupings, apportionment would not be difficult. In practice, however, because of variations in registration and voting turnout, the relationship is not constant.

Constitutional or electoral malapportionment must not be confused with gerrymandering—a form of arbitrary districting used to benefit the party that at a given time controls the apportionment process. Gerrymandering takes its name from the governor of Massachusetts Elbridge Gerry (1744–1814), who recognized the possibility of influencing electoral outcomes by manipulating the boundaries of electoral districts (critics charged that one of the districts he designed resembled a salamander).

Elbridge Gerry, delegate to the U.S. Continental Congress and namesake of the practice of gerrymandering. Hulton Archive/ Getty Images

Gerrymandering involves concentrating large percentages of the opposite party's votes into a few districts and drawing the boundaries of the other districts in such a way that the gerrymandering party wins them all, even though the majority, or, in multiparty elections, the plurality, is relatively small. A widely cited example of gerrymandering occurred in Northern Ireland, where districts were drawn to maximize the representation of Unionists prior to the imposition of direct rule by the British Parliament in 1972.

Gerrymandering is a common political tactic throughout the world. Political parties prefer "safe" districts to those that are competitive. By not contesting seriously in the other party's safe districts, by maintaining one's own safe districts, and by carving competitive districts up in such a way that one's own party is favoured (generally through legislative apportionment), party managers advance their own party's interests but often harm other social, economic, and political interests that need representation. Although gerrymandering is common and generally regarded as legal, gerrymandering based on race has been ruled unconstitutional in the United States.

VOTING PRACTICES

There is a direct relationship between the size of an electorate and the formalization and standardization of its voting practices. In very small voting groups, in which political encounters are face-to-face and the members are bound together by ties of friendship or common experience, political discussion is mostly informal and may not even require formal voting, because the "sense of the meeting" emerges from the group's deliberations. An issue is discussed until a solution emerges to which all participants can agree or, at least, from which any one participant will not dissent.

BAKER V. CARR

The U.S. Supreme Court's decision in the legal case *Baker* v. *Carr* (1962) forced the Tennessee legislature to reapportion itself on the basis of population. Traditionally, particularly in the South, the populations of rural areas had been overrepresented in legislatures in proportion to those of urban and suburban areas. Prior to the Baker case, the Supreme Court had refused to intervene in influence of *Baker* v. *Carr* apportionment cases. In *Colegrove* v. *Green* (1946), for example, the court said apportionment was a "political thicket" into which the judiciary should not intrude. In the Baker case, however, the court held that each vote should carry equal weight regardless of the voter's place of residence. Thus the legislature of Tennessee had violated the constitutionally guaranteed right of equal protection. Chief Justice Earl Warren described this decision as the most important case decided after his appointment to the court in 1953.

Citing the Baker case as a precedent, the court held in *Reynolds* v. *Sims* (1964) that both houses of bicameral legislatures had to be apportioned according to population. It remanded numerous other apportionment cases to lower courts for reconsideration in light of the Baker and Reynolds decisions. As a result, virtually every state legislature was reapportioned, ultimately causing the political power in most state legislatures to shift from rural to urban areas.

By contrast, in modern mass electorates, in which millions of individual votes are aggregated into a collective choice, formalization and standardization of voting practices and vote counting are required to ensure that the outcome is valid, reliable, and legitimate. Validity means that the collective choice in fact expresses the will of the electorate, reliability refers to each vote's being accurately recorded and effectively counted, and legitimacy means that the criteria of validity and reliability have been met, so that the result of the voting is acceptable and provides authoritative guidelines in subsequent political conduct. In some countries that hold elections, observers have reported irregularities in the counting of votes and have questioned the legitimacy of the results. For example, one study of the U.S. presidential election of 2000 found that millions of votes were uncounted as a result of outdated election equipment, registration errors, and other problems, which led some critics to argue that the outcome was illegitimate.

Routinized and standardized electoral practices in mass electorates were developed beginning in the mid 19th century. Their development was as much a corollary of the growth of rapid communication through telephone and telegraph as of the growth of the electorate and rational insistence on making electoral processes fair and equitable. Nevertheless, electoral practices around the world differ a great deal, depending not just on formal institutional arrangements but even more on a country's political culture.

SECRET VOTING

Once suffrage rights had been extended to masses of voters who, in theory, were assumed to be equal, open voting was no longer tolerable, precisely because it could and often did involve undue influence, ranging from hidden persuasion and bribery to intimidation, coercion, and punishment. Equality, at least in voting, was not something given but something that had to be engineered: the secrecy of the vote was a first and necessary administrative step toward the one person, one vote principle. Equality in voting was possible only if each vote was formally independent of every other vote, and this suggested the need for strict secrecy.

Often called the Australian ballot because of its use in the Australian states of Victoria and South Australia, secret voting gradually was adopted as the norm. Its eventual adoption was largely due to increased literacy and, at the cultural level, to the spread of individualistic norms of privacy and anonymity to certain classes of the population, notably peasants and workers. Traditionally, these groups took their cues from those they accepted as superiors or from their peers. Secret voting required learning to free oneself as a citizen from customary associations and from pressures for conformity. Even in the contemporary world, developing countries with low literacy rates and with strong ties to tradition were slow to adopt secret voting.

Secret voting dramatically reduces the possibility of undue influence on the voter. Without it, influence can range from the outright purchase of votes to social chastisement or economic sanctions. Although laws exist in most countries to prohibit and punish the purchase or sale of votes, the introduction of secret voting has not wholly eliminated bribery.

Informal social pressures on the voter are probably unavoidable and, in some respects, useful in reducing political rootlessness and contributing to political stability. However, secrecy in voting permits voters to break away from their social moorings and gives them a considerable degree of independence if they wish to take advantage of this electoral freedom. As a result, it becomes ever more difficult for interest groups—whether labour unions, farmers' organizations, commercial or industrial associations, ethnic leadership groups, or even criminal syndicates—to "deliver the vote." The extent to which "deviant voting" occurs depends partly on the degree of rigidity in the social structure. In countries where caste or class barriers are strong or where traditional social, economic, religious, or regional cleavages remain in place, deviant voting is less likely than in countries where there is significant social mobility and where political conflicts cut across traditional social cleavages.

BALLOTING

The ballot makes secret voting possible. Its initial use seems to have been as a means to reduce irregularities and deception in elections. However, this objective could be achieved only if the ballot was not supplied by the voter himself, as was the case in much early voting by secret ballot, or by political parties, as is still the case in some countries. Ballot procedures differ widely, ranging from marking the names of preferred candidates to crossing out those not preferred or writing in the names of persons who are not formal candidates. Some ballots require the selection of one or more candidates or parties or both, and others require the preferential ordering of a number of candidates.

It is generally believed that the nature of the ballot influences a voter's choice. In jurisdictions where electors are called upon to vote not only for higher offices but also for a multitude of local positions and where the election may include propositions in the nature of referenda, the length of the ballot can affect the results. Overwhelmed by a ballot's length, voters may be discouraged from expressing their preferences for candidates of whom they have not heard, or from deciding on propositions that they do not understand. For example, in some U.S. jurisdictions, participation is often lower in contests for county coroners, tax assessors, and other local positions for which there is often little coverage in the media. Election data show a rapid decline from votes cast for higher offices to those cast for lower offices and referendum-type propositions, a phenomenon referred to as ballot roll-off.

Ballot position also has an effect on the votes cast for particular candidates, especially in the absence of cues as to party affiliation or other identifications. The first position on the ballot may be favoured, and on long ballots both first and last names may benefit, with candidates in the middle of the ballot suffering slightly. Ballot position is likely to have its greatest impact in nonpartisan elections, primaries, and elections for minor offices.

The manner in which candidates are listed—by party column or by office bloc—is likely to affect election outcomes. On party-column ballots, it is possible to vote a "straight ticket" for all of a party's candidates by entering a single mark, though voting for individual candidates is usually possible. Conversely, on the office-bloc ballot,

A Broward County, Fla., Canvassing Board member closely inspects one of the state's punch-card ballots in 2001. The ballots were at the centre of controversy over the 2000 presidential election. Robert King/Getty Images

voters choose individual candidates grouped by office rather than party, which discourages voting exclusively for members of one party, though some jurisdictions that use the office-bloc ballot allow voters to cast a straight ticket.

Electoral results also can be dramatically affected when some voters find the ballot difficult to use or understand. Indeed, a study in the U.S. state of Florida found that an allegedly confusing ballot design in one county and improperly punched ballots across the state may well have been critical to the overall outcome of the national presidential election in 2000. The analysis, which highlighted the problems associated with various voting methods and the disparate distribution of voting technologies according to socioeconomic status (i.e., wealthier areas generally had more advanced technology and fewer invalidated ballots), spurred extensive debate about election reform.

The type of ballot can have important consequences for the operation of government, especially in systems with separated powers and federal territorial organization. If different offices are controlled by different parties, the governmental process may be marked by greater conflict than would otherwise be the case.

The introduction of voting machines and computer technology has not substantially changed the balloting process, though it generally has made it faster and more economical. Voting machines are not without problems, in that they may marginally depress the level of voting owing to improper use, a problem that can be overcome through improved machines and voter education.

COMPULSORY VOTING

In some countries, notably Australia and Belgium, electoral participation is legally required, and nonvoters can face fines. The concept of compulsory voting reflects a strain in democratic theory in which voting is considered not merely a right but a duty. Its purpose is to ensure the electoral equality of all social groups. However, whether created through laws or through social pressure, it is doubtful that high voter turnout is a good indication of an electorate's capability for intelligent social choice. On the other hand, high rates of abstention or differential rates of abstention by different social classes are not necessarily signs of satisfaction with governmental processes and policies and in fact may indicate the contrary.

ELECTORAL ABUSES

Corrupt electoral practices are not limited to bribery or voter intimidation. They include disseminating scurrilous rumours and false campaign propaganda, tampering with election machinery by stuffing ballot boxes with fraudulent returns, counting or reporting the vote dishonestly, and disregarding electoral outcomes by incumbent officeholders (e.g., by mobilizing the military to thwart an election loss). The existence of these practices depends more on a population's adherence to political civility and the democratic ethos than on legal prohibitions and sanctions.

The integrity of the electoral process can be maintained by a variety of devices and practices, including a permanent and up-to-date register of voters and procedures designed to make the registration process as simple as possible. In most jurisdictions, elections are held on a single day rather than on staggered days. Polling hours in all localities are generally the same, and opening and closing hours are fixed and announced, so that voters have an equal opportunity to participate. Polling stations are operated by presumably disinterested government officials or polling clerks under governmental supervision.

Political party agents or party workers are given an opportunity to observe the polling process, which enables them to challenge irregularities and prevent abuses. Efforts are made to maintain order in polling stations, directly through police protection or indirectly through such practices as closing bars and liquor stores. The act of voting itself takes place in voting booths to protect privacy. Votes are counted and often recounted by tellers, who are watched by party workers to ensure an honest count. The transmission of voting results from local polling stations to central election headquarters is safeguarded and checked.

PARTICIPATION IN ELECTIONS

Electoral participation rates depend on many factors, including the type of electoral system, the social groupings to which voters belong, the voters' personalities and beliefs, their places of residence, and a host of other idiosyncratic factors.

The level and type of election have a great impact on the rate of electoral participation. Electoral turnout is greater in national than in state or provincial elections, and greater in the latter than in local elections. If local elections are held concurrently with provincial or national elections, generally a higher voter turnout is achieved than for nonconcurrent elections. Whether an election is partisan or nonpartisan also affects turnout, as fewer people participate in nonpartisan elections. Supporters of political parties vote more often than those without a partisan identification. Participation is also usually greater in candidate elections than in noncandidate elections such as referenda. There is evidence that elections based on proportional representation have higher electoral turnouts than majority or plurality elections. Voter turnout tends to be depressed in noncompetitive or safe electoral districts and elevated in competitive ones. The perceived closeness of an electoral contest and the degree of ideological polarization between parties or candidates can affect the competitiveness of the election and consequently its turnout. The frequency of elections is also related to voter participation, as fewer people tend to participate in countries where elections are more frequent.

Technicalities in the electoral law may disenfranchise many potential voters. For example, people who change their legal residence may temporarily lose their vote because of residence requirements for voters in their new electoral district. Complicated voter-registration procedures, combined with a high level of geographic mobility, significantly reduce the size of the active electorate in the United States, whereas in many other countries the size of the electorate is maximized by government-initiated registration immediately prior to an election. Voter registration in the United States is largely left to the initiative of individuals and political parties, though attempts to increase voter registration were made in the 1990s through the implementation of "motor-voter laws," which allowed citizens to register to vote when they received or renewed their driver's licenses.

Relatively low levels of electoral participation are associated with low levels of education, occupational status, and income. Those groups in society that have been most recently enfranchised also tend to vote at lower rates. For a significant period of time in the 20th century, women voted less frequently than men, though the difference had been erased by the end of the century in most countries. The rates of participation of racial minorities are generally lower than those of majority groups, and members of the working class vote less frequently than members of the middle class. In many countries, participation by young people is significantly lower than that of older people.

The failure of certain types of people to vote in elections has important implications. Most analyses have found that if all eligible voters cast ballots, the balance of electoral power would favour the recently enfranchised and less-privileged members of society.

A small group of people are conscientious nonvoters. Others, perceiving the vote more as an instrument of censure than of support, may not vote because they are satisfied with the current government. This group of voluntary nonvoters is also small, however. In fact, nonvoters generally are less satisfied with the political status quo than are voters. The vote is a rather blunt and ineffectual instrument for expressing dissatisfaction, and nonvoting is more likely to be symptomatic of alienation from the political system than of satisfaction with it.

A number of random factors influence individual participation in specific elections. Election campaigns vary in their intensity. A crisis atmosphere may induce a large number of people to vote on one occasion, whereas on another the chance to vote for an extremist candidate may increase the participation of the normally uninterested. Even the weather can affect election turnout.

Voter participation varies from country to country. For example, approximately half of the voting-age population participates in presidential elections in the United States. In contrast, many European countries have participation rates exceeding 80 percent. Even within Europe, however, participation varies significantly. Research has suggested a long-term decline in turnout at national elections in western democracies since the 1970s. It seems most likely that this is a consequence of partisan dealignment (i.e., a weakening of partisan identification), the erosion of social cleavages based on class and religion, and increasing voter discontent.

INFLUENCES ON VOTING BEHAVIOUR

The electoral choices of voters are influenced by a range of factors, especially social-group identity, which helps to forge enduring partisan identification. In addition, voters are to a greater or lesser extent susceptible to the influence of more short-term and contingent factors such as campaign events, issues, and candidate appeals. In particular, the perceived governing competence of candidates and political parties often weighs heavily on voters' choices.

Research suggests that, through partisan dealignment, the proportion of voters in Western democracies who retain their long-term partisan identities has been reduced. In conjunction with the declining impact of social-group influences, voter choice is now more heavily affected by short-term factors relevant to specific election campaigns. This shift from long-term predisposition to short-term evaluation has been facilitated in part by the phenomenon of "cognitive mobilization," a supposed enhancement of the political independence and intelligence of voters who are both better educated and better informed than earlier generations. Nevertheless, many independents and nonvoters are poorly informed politically and relatively uninterested and uninvolved in politics. Whether cognitively mobilized or not, however, independent voters are often a decisive factor in elections. If elections are to be competitive, and if control of the government is to alternate between parties or coalitions of parties, then some voters must switch party support from election to election. New voters and independent voters, therefore, provide a vital source of change in democratic politics.

This book has explored a few of the basic formal and informal institutions of political life in modern democratic countries and examined how they give expression to the preferences and opinions of the electorate and of its various component groups, classes, and communities. One informal and ubiquitous institution, the political party, is an essential element of any large representative democracy because it enables segments of the electorate with broadly similar views to select and promote candidates who will protect their interests. Political parties also serve to identify the political orientation of candidates for the voting public and ensure, by enforcing party discipline, that representatives in the legislature do not support policies that are radically at odds with the platforms on which they were elected. The fact that successful and established political parties are not internally fully democratic, tending to be ruled by cliques, is considered a necessary evil, given the benefits to democracy that political parties are thought to bring.

Like political parties, interest groups are a means of organizing the political efforts of like-minded individuals and groups. Unlike parties, however, interest groups do not seek political power but aim instead to influence government policy in ways that benefit their members or that further their particular causes. To this end, and depending on their resources, they may lobby elected officials, contribute money to their reelection campaigns, provide legal research and analysis, and draft model legislation that representatives may then incorporate into bills introduced in the legislature. Many interest groups exist solely to protect the financial interests or political privileges of their members—though they almost always profess dedication to the public interest or to some other higher cause. Such groups are usually regarded as harmful to democracy because they typically succeed only to the extent that they effect changes in government policy that benefit their members at the expense of the public or the country, and because their goals are frequently inconsistent with the preferences of a majority of the electorate as expressed at the voting booth and through surveys of public opinion.

Political parties and individual politicians in democratic countries naturally pay close attention to public opinion. Despite the conventional idea that wise candidates and elected officials tend to formulate their platforms and policies to reflect public opinion as revealed in polls and focus groups, it is common for political campaigns and government press offices to attempt to influence public opinion in order to generate support for agendas that are largely predetermined. For this purpose they may take advantage of sophisticated techniques of message crafting that are used by advertising, marketing, and public relations firms to influence the purchasing decisions of consumers or to improve the public images of corporations and foreign governments. Although public opinion is thus not immune to manipulation by people who profess to be guided by it, not every element of it is easily changed, and it ultimately represents an important limitation on what government leaders can do. Thus public officials will often seek to defend (or at least not to undermine) policies and programs that opinion polls have shown to be widely popular.

The formal (i.e., constitutionally established) institution through which the electorate makes known its political preferences is the election. National political systems that incorporate regular popular elections are a fairly recent phenomenon, having first arisen in North America and Europe in the 18th and 19th centuries. The institution is obviously at the core of modern representative democracy, for it is the basic means by which the people express and enforce their political will. Elections serve democracy in other ways, e.g., by providing a public forum (in competitive elections) in which important issues may be discussed, thereby helping voters to make informed decisions, and by conferring legitimacy upon the government, thereby contributing to the stability of the political system.

Despite the enormous importance of elections, participation in them varies widely, depending on the level of the election (e.g., national, regional, or local), its competitiveness, the degree of partisanship or ideological division it displays, and the general political culture, among many other factors. In some countries, large segments of the electorate regularly fail to vote because they believe that none of the candidates or parties takes their interests seriously or because they feel that the political system itself effectively excludes them, despite its formal democratic character. In other countries, regular and widespread electoral abuses and corruption may convince many people that their votes simply do not matter. Notwithstanding the continuing problem of electoral participation, the number of countries in which regular popular elections took place increased dramatically in the second half of the 20th century, and this trend seems likely to continue in the early 21st century.

apportionment To divide or separate into sections according to plan.

ballot The action or system of secret voting.

cadre A core group of people with a unifying relationship, particularly a group of leaders who support a revolutionary government.

caucus A closed meeting attended by members of a particular political party, typically to select candidates or decide on party policy.

clique An exclusive group of people who hold similar interests, goals, or purposes.

coalition A temporary alliance of distinct parties, persons, or states for joint action.

constituency A body of citizens entitled to elect a representative.

egalitarian Of or pertaining to a social philosophy advocating the removal of inequalities among people.

electoral college A body of representatives from each state that is responsible for selecting the president of the United States.

fascist One who has a tendency toward or actual exercise of strong autocratic or dictatorial control.

feudal Of or pertaining to a political and economic system in medieval Europe based on the power of landholders over their tenants, who worked the land on which they lived to benefit the landowner.

gerrymander To divide an area into election districts that benefit one political party.

heterogeneous Consisting of diverse or mixed ingredients or constituents.

ideology The theories and beliefs shared by a group of people with similar sociopolitical views.

paternalistic Of or concerning a system under which an authority attempts to meet the needs or regulate the conduct of those under its control.

plebiscite A vote by which the people of an entire country or district express an opinion for or against a proposal, form of government or a leader.

plurality In politics, an excess of votes over those cast for an opposing candidate.

propaganda Information disseminated to sway others toward a cause.

referendum The practice of submitting to popular vote a measure passed on or proposed by a legislative body or by popular initiative.

suffrage The right to vote; also the exercise of such a right.

POLITICAL PARTIES

Robert Michels, *Political Parties: A Sociological Study of the Oligarchical Tendencies of Modern Democracies* (1915, reissued 1978; originally published in German, 1911), provides the first modern theory of political parties, based largely on the example of German social democracy. Reference works providing world coverage of political parties include George E. Delury and Jayne Weisblatt (eds.), *World Encyclopedia of Political Systems and Parties*, 4th ed. (2006); and Alan J. Day (ed.), Political *Parties of the World*, 5th ed. (2002).

INTEREST GROUPS

The most comprehensive reference on interest group studies is Clive S. Thomas (ed.), *Research Guide to U.S. and International Interest Groups* (2004). A good treatment of interest groups in U.S. politics at the national level is Jeffrey M. Berry and Clyde Wilcox, *Interest Group Society*, 4th ed. (2007). More than 300 interest groups in the United States are profiled in Immanuel Ness, *Encyclopedia of Interest Groups and Lobbyists in the United States*, 2 vol. (2000). Interest groups in international and transnational politics are discussed in Jackie Smith, Charles Chatfield, and Ron Pagnucco, *Transnational Social Movements and Global Politics* (1997).

PUBLIC OPINION

The history of public opinion is traced in John R. Zaller, *The Nature and Origins of Mass Opinion* (1992); and Slavko Splichal, *Public Opinion: Developments and Controversies in the Twentieth Century* (1999).

Excellent summaries of polling theory and application are found in Sherry Devereaux Ferguson, *Researching the Public Opinion Environment: Theories and Methods* (2000); and Paul J. Lavrakas and Michael W. Traugott, *Election Polls, the News Media, and Democracy* (2000).

Defenses of the polling process by eminent practitioners are Leo Bogart, *Polls and the Awareness of Public Opinion*, 2nd ed. (1988); Albert H. Cantril, *The Opinion Connection* (1991); and Daniel Yankelovich, *Coming to Public Judgment* (1991). Academic critiques of polling include Benjamin Ginsberg, *The Captive Public: How Mass Opinion Promotes State Power* (1986); and John Lukacs, *Democracy and Populism: Fear and Hatred* (2005).

ELECTIONS

A readable, comprehensive overview of electoral institutions is David M. Farrell, *Electoral Systems: A Comparative Introduction* (2001). The impact of electoral systems on party systems is analyzed in Arend Lijphart et al., *Electoral Systems and Party Systems: A Study of Twenty-seven Democracies, 1945–1990* (1994). The significance for democratic theory of electoral arrangements is considered in Richard S. Katz, *Democracy and Elections* (1997).

Analyses of referenda and direct democracy can be found in David Butler and Austin Ranney (eds.), *Referendums Around the World: The Growing Use of Direct*

Democracy (1994); and Ian Budge, *The New Challenge of Direct Democracy* (1996).

Developments in voting behaviour are discussed in Samuel L. Popkin, *The Reasoning Voter: Communication and Persuasion in Presidential Campaigns*, 2nd ed. (1994); Geoffrey Evans (ed.), *The End of Class Politics?: Class Voting in Comparative Context* (1999); and Samuel Merrill III and Bernard Grofman, *A Unified Theory of Voting: Directional and Proximity Spatial Models* (1999).